READER RESPONSES

I'm reluctant to call Worship of Hollow Gods a literary novel, but it is from the standpoint of language, language that is fresh and new, colorful and extraordinary but never cliché or ordinary. It is a beautiful appreciation of the power of words to evoke images. It's a rich look at the protagonist's heritage, mingled with the family saga, the family dynamics of a household, neighborhood, multi-generational, close-knit community joined by duty and heritage. From the view of a male-child we learn to see with new eyes and new heart. *Worship of Hollow Gods* is unputdownable. It's a wonderful evocative read.

—Billie A. Williams, Best-Selling,
Award Winning Mystery/Suspense Author

I can barely move after reading your story. I was crying, nearly overwhelmed by all the anguish and heartbreak. *Worship of Hollow Gods* is a masterpiece. Everyone should read it because everyone has lived it, each in a singular way, and by reading it they'll be better able to understand, and maybe even forgive and love.

—Art Klein, Best-Selling Book of the Month Club Author
and former Vice President of Marketing for
The New York Times Corporation

James Sniechowski's poignant snapshot of growing up in a Polish-Catholic family in Detroit shows how the disappointments, beliefs, and events of the past seep into the marrow of future generations. Within our bones dwell the struggles of our ancestors, which we carry throughout our lives. It is a haunting portrait of the power of familial bonds that forever hold us tight and shape our destiny.

—Susan Heim, co-editor "Chicken Soup for the Soul:
Devotional Stories for Women"

Seeing the family interactions through the eyes of a nine-year-old-boy, this story unravels the dynamics of the boy's family exposing feelings, emotions, and family secrets. Throughout the book Sniechowski opens avenues that the reader may relate to in their own family. Toward the end of the story I began to understand the author's choice of title and how one can relate to this family and their relationships. This is definitely a recommended read.

—Dee Owen - bookread-mumswritings.blogspot.com

Worship of Hollow Gods is a nearly perfect novel. Descriptions are so detailed and realistic and the dialogue so resonant that you are immediately drawn in and glued there. Amazingly, even though you are often submerged in the main character's thoughts and emotions, the book maintains the story action and keeps you turning the page. I highly recommend this insightful and beautifully crafted book.

—Signe A. Dayhoff, author of "Growing Up 'Unacceptable': How Katherine Hepburn Rescued Me"

Hollow Gods is incredible! A gripping, vivid portrayal of the human spirit. Through beautiful language, the characters stepped off the page; each person's unconscious pain woven in with masterful craftsmanship. Sniechowski's writing is brilliant and engaging, at times poetic and always moving, brightly illustrating the bittersweet reality of life. Stunning every step of the way.

—Kevin Eyres, Northern CA

From the soul of a nine-year-old-boy comes the tale of a family few will ever come to know without reading this wonderful story. Sniechowski is a talented writer, already a master of ticklish phrasing that makes a novel special.

—Kevin Gerard - award winning author of the Diego's Dragon fantasy series

All I can say is, "WOW!" It is brilliant! Wonderful descriptions, perfect dialogue, resonant and so realistic.

—Mercy St. Pierre, St. George, Utah

I LOVE this book ... whenever I put it down I feel like I have to hurry up and get back to the book or I'll miss what the family is doing. Excellent job painting pictures with the words - I feel like I'm right there.

—Tonja Johnson, Detroit, MI

Jim's book is chock full of images that as I read I saw the movie. He is such a skilled writer and I can feel what he is saying. What a splendid way to get to know him, through his story. What an accomplishment to write a good visual book skillfully AND the kind that needs to be made into a movie. WOW!

—Wendy Lucas, Senior Real Estate Specialist, Virginia Beach, VA

Most families take their dark underbelly for granted, but Sniechowski takes us inside the mystery of his own early roots and invites us to join in the experience. Flawlessly written with compassion and ferocity, it's a soul-stirring read.

—Kyla Nelson, Santa Monica, CA

I could totally relate. Detroit or The Bronx, it didn't matter. Polish Catholic or Polish Jewish, it also didn't matter. Instead of names like Alexandr, or Julli or Chez, my same memories are of Rose, Shirley, Becky and Mamie. The card games were exactly the same. So similar, and so nostalgic. Thank you for writing the book. I knew it would be well written, but I had no idea it would strike such a personal cord.

—Gary Goldberg, Financial Advisor, Suffern, NY

I love the story. It's so interesting to get the feel of peasant, immigrant experience, assimilating into a foreign culture like the acceptance of fate, as within Sniechowski's grandparents arranged marriage, a concept we normally don't equate with the United States; though, obviously common back then, as a way to maintain one's native sub-culture within the dominate culture. A wonderful read!

—Jane Wynes, Henderson, NV

A compelling story, the roots of mother-bound loyalty and father-fear drive the reader to find out what's going to happen at the end. It's a read I thoroughly enjoyed.

—Josh Lance, Las Vegas NV

Just finished Sniechowski's book. WOW!!! What a ride. The author's family was brought to life - full on and in living color! What an insight into Jim's early childhood. The ending got me - didn't see that coming. Still reeling from it all and the author left me wanting to know more. Is there a movie script in the making? Found myself wanting to hug "Little Jimmy/Jimush."

—Duke Stroud, Actor and Legal Presentation Coach, Pasadena, CA

Worship
of Hollow Gods

JAMES SNIECHOWSKI

Inspired by Real Life Events

All rights reserved. This book is protected under the copyright laws of the United States of America. No part of this publication may be reproduced, stored in a retrieval system, or transmitted in any form or by any means—electronic, mechanical, photocopying, recording, or otherwise—without the prior written permission of the publisher.

This book is a work of autobiographical fiction. Characters, names, locations, events and incidents have been disguised to protect the privacy of any remaining persons still living.

ISBN: 978-0-9913172-0-2 print
Second Edition
eISBN: 978-0-9913172-1-9

Cover Design: Alexander Von Ness
Cover Photo Credit: m930605/Flickr

274 Redwood Shores Pkwy #716, Redwood City, CA 94065
Copyright © 2018

For My Wife and Partner
Judith Sherven
Without Whom This Would Not Be

And For My Detroit Family
Who Believed in an Afterlife
And For Whose Sake
I Sincerely Hope One Exists

Worship *of* Hollow Gods

Prologue

The words "leaving home" are central to my Leaving Home Trilogy. Leaving Home is most often understood as leaving a place of residence, more commonly known as your home. But in the Leaving Home Trilogy they take on a very different meaning. Every child grows up in the emotional home of their early years, and every child's initial response to life is based on the emotional condition of that first home. An obvious example would be growing up in a home of violence leaving the impression of a violent world the child has come to expect and needs to protect itself from. As the early expectations are experienced internally over and over they become habit, and as habit they recede into the unconscious mind from where they dictate many of the attitudes, beliefs, and behaviors of a person's ongoing life. On the other hand, if the home is one of care and support and respect for who the child is the child grows up into a world he or she can trust and thrive in. For any person to leave home no matter their age and no matter their early conditions, it is precisely the world of the unconscious impressions and judgments that every person unavoidably takes with them into their later life. The "Leaving Home Trilogy" is a three-book fictional series about how the lead character, Jim, struggles to free himself from the grip of his own unconscious restraints and the discoveries he and the reader make along the way.

Thanks,
Jim Sniechowski

The Family Gathers

"Shot and a beer," Uncle Bo shouted as he walked through the back door, his wife, Irene, in tow.

My mother, Helen, Bo's younger sister, had the order ready. She'd filled that same order so many times it had become reflexive: a two-ounce jigger of Seagram's Seven Crown and an uncapped bottle of Stroh's.

She'd stashed the dish drainer beneath the kitchen sink—as she always did when her brothers and their wives gathered for a Friday night of pinochle and poker—converting the surface into a makeshift bar stocked with bottles of cold Stroh's, in 1950 Detroit's most popular beer, and a couple of fifths of Seagram's Seven Crown, the only whisky my family would drink.

The white porcelain sink top, discolored by grease and food stains and covered with a worn and fading black and white cross-hatched dish towel, functioned as the only surface in our 8 x 10 kitchen appropriately profane to serve as the liquor bar. The yellowish-white Formica table, the only other usable surface, was considered sacred in our very Catholic household, because bread—rye, white, and pumpernickel—wrapped in cellophane or butcher paper and almost always present on the table, represented the body of Christ. Any alcohol placed on the table would strip that sacrosanct surface of its authority to function as a dwelling place for the divine and desecrate the very idea of the holy.

Bo raised his shot glass, tipping it slightly toward everyone in the room, and threw the Seven Crown past his lips to the back of his throat and down. After the stinging Bourbon pushed his lips to a point, a triumphant smile, like a post-eclipsed sun, followed, and he burst out, "Shiiiit," wiping his lips with the back of his hand. "*Cholernie dobre*," Polish for "That's damn good."

The members of my mother's family, surname *Niemiec* (Nee-mick), prided themselves in being pure-bred Poles, my maternal grandparents having arrived in Detroit without detour or diversion straight from the farm fields of the Old Country. I heard them say, again and again, "We are not mongrels. Not Germans, not Russians, not Ukranians. Poles, that's who we are. One hundred percent."

And Poles they were. Archetypical Poles: tall broad foreheads with square faces that boxed in their ruddy cheeks, round noses, full lips, and slightly angular chins. Their eyes ranged from an ethereal blue to a piercing black and, in my family's case, set off against thick hair varying from soft and flowing light-brown to coarse and wiry black. Bo's wife, Irene, born of non-Niemiec blood stock, was a natural blond.

"*Dziękuję*, Helcha." Bo used the affectionate name, Helcha, her older brothers had given her and as he passed her on his way to the living room he took the Stroh's. "Thanks."

"It's nothing," my mother smiled. "*To nic*." Most of my relatives slipped effortlessly from Polish to English and vice versa.

My mother entered the world of her family like a bookmark flagging her place behind the first three boys baptized Jerzy (Jerry), Julek (he did not like nicknames but everyone called him Julli) and Bogusz (Bo), and ahead of two more, Arek (Ari) and Czeslaw (Chez). She was number four.

Birth order is supposed to have causal and life-long effects on personality development. Those who arrive in the fourth slot are supposed to struggle with issues of trust and isolation yet suffer, at the same time, from a deep desire to belong, traits that buffeted my mother back and forth between withdrawal and need. Astrology claims that those whose life path is represented by the number four are supposed to be gifted with the talent of making things work, an aptitude my mother missed, leaving her dependent and resentful. But most of all her fourth place descendancy into the Niemiec family had less to do with how she ended up identity-wise than having been surrounded by and immersed in her brothers' boisterous and brawling testosterone.

She'd ingested the Old World prejudice of a woman's place as second to men so completely that her deference was not a submission but a belief in the rightness of male superiority which relegated her to the standing of a servant to peasants. Years later when I asked her how she felt about this she'd say, "Well, that's just the way it was then."

"How the hell are you, Helch?" Irene asked kissing my mother's cheek.

"Good, good," my mother's predictable response. She handed Irene what the women drank, Seven and Seven, a mix of two ounces of Seven Crown and the rest 7UP.

Although Irene was Polish and Catholic and she'd gained access into the Niemiec clan through her marriage to Bo, still there was something not quite right about her. She didn't live in the neighborhood. Her face was long and not square. Her eyes, on occasion, suggested the oriental almond shape rather than the round European. And it was rumored that her mother may have had some Russian blood in her background.

In spite of her legitimate and genuine adherence to Roman Catholicism, some of the old women fretted, without any proof whatsoever, that she might be Eastern Catholic: *Prawosławie* (Byzantine), a word that sent shivers through the base of a devout Polish Catholic's neck because it always sounded fishy and frightening. After all, the Eastern Orthodox Church didn't have Popes. They had Patriarchs with names like Dorotheus, Theophylact, Eleutherius—Patriarchs of Antioch; Rastko, Predislav, Makalje—Patriarchs of Serbia; Proterius, Dioscorus, and Onopsus—Patriarchs of Alexandria; and, perhaps the worst, Nikon, Theognostus, Joasaphus—Patriarchs of Moscow and all the Russias. Who ever heard of such names?

Popes had real names like Peter, Martin, Gregory, Leo, Pius, and Paul. Maybe not solidly Polish names, but names you could trust.

And the Popes were not Pope of this or that. They were "just plain Pope."

Because Irene's pedigree was suspect, and because of all the women she was the best poker player which, in our community, was a sign of a mysterious aberration—women weren't supposed to be good at cards and they were sure not supposed to beat the men which she enjoyed and did not let them forget—Irene always seemed to exude a sense of something undefined and irreverent. When the older, habitually-subservient women gathered among themselves, they'd say, "She's not a proper woman." They couldn't begin to understand and certainly would never accept her unavoidable and sometimes showy otherness which scared them. Instead they blamed her strangeness on her independence, her sense of freedom and fun, and some even whispered, "I think she's Russian," which was the same as saying "Godless."

"*Co nowego, Irenka?*" my mother asked.

"What's new? Same old shit, you know." Irene sighed, revealing the gap between her two front teeth.

No one else had a gap, adding to her otherness. Sometimes I caught myself staring into that blackness, a portal into something mysterious, more mysterious than I could imagine, and more mysterious than was good for me, so I forced myself not to look.

"I know. I know," my mother nodded. "Same old, same old."

My mother seemed to possess a genetic quirk, a gene specifically adapted for compliance. So she gave her relatives, gave most people, what they wanted to hear.

"That son of a bitch of a foreman of mine was a real pain in the ass today." Irene spit toward the floor without a trace of spittle leaving her lips, a denunciation she'd learned from the Old Country women.

My mother didn't like cussing. It frightened her: both because of its sinful nature, and because it was so aggressive. But when it came from Irene's mouth she allowed herself to be entertained by it. Of her five sisters-in-law, Irene, whom my mother secretly envied, was the only one who cussed unselfconsciously. Profanity found a home in her mouth like the Stroh's bottle in her husband's hand; unforced, unaffected, organic.

"He had a bug up his ass all day. Wouldn't pass a damn thing I did, you know?"

"*Tsk, tsk, tsk.*" My mother's concern was laced with contempt: two ounces of concern for Irene and the rest, contempt for that son-of-a-bitch of a foreman. My mother knew about not being valued.

"He turned everything back," Irene sipped. "I had to keep doing things over and over again, the son of a bitch."

Irene had worked at the Ford Motor Company during the Second World War. As one of Rosie the Riveter's brigade, she proved her mettle and stayed on once the war had ended. She loved working for her own money and she could give the men as good as she got. Some of the men enjoyed tussling with her, but others were most often afraid and kept their distance. A woman with her own mind was not something they were accustomed to or knew how to handle.

My mother's concern for the abuse Irene claimed to have suffered masked her envy. She'd wanted a factory job before she married even though her paycheck would never have been her own because she would have been ordered to deposit all of it into the family kitty, without any allowance. She knew that. But mostly she'd wanted a job because of the romantic images she'd invented about the glamour of working in a factory, the characters she'd meet, and the colorful life she would enjoy. She charmed herself into a persistent yearning until she asked permission and her mother's condemning frown said it all. "Women don't make money. They keep house. *Nie wolno*, not allowed."

Irene peered into her Seven and Seven, brooding, her face dark and distant, until a raucous laugh exploded from her belly inspiring her to throw back a gulp. "Ah, what the hell. Someday..." she winked at my mother as she brought her forefinger and middle finger together making a scissors gesture.

"Ahhhh," my mother hissed. "*Wstyd*, Irene. Shame."

Undaunted and encouraged by my mother's squeamishness Irene kept her fingers snipping until my mother could no longer suppress her laughter.

"Enough, Irenka. Enough."

"How about pinking shears?" She poked her scissoring fingers into my mother's ribs. "We'll give him such a snipping. That'll show him, the son of a bitch."

They laughed and squealed like twelve-year-old co-conspirators anticipating the results of a too tooooo delicious prank.

Their salacious rage spread through our Catholic kitchen like the Sacred Garden's ancient serpent: slipping behind the refrigerator, edging under the stove, coiling around the homemade cotton curtains, lounging atop the white metal cover over the radiator in the corner, causing the Christ on the cross hanging on the wall above the table to squirm. At nine years old I couldn't have told you what was going on but I sure did feel its pulse and enjoyed its gutsiness.

Into that swirl of id and giddy sin stepped my cousin Janice, framed in the jamb of the back door, haloed by that mid-July evening's lingering light streaming in through the windows of the closed-in porch behind her. In that glow, she looked like many of the saints I'd seen depicted on holy picture cards parishioners used for contemplation or as book marks in their prayer missals.

I'd long been drawn into Janice's aura, helpless to hold back my deepening infatuation. At the point of no return I surrendered sinking deeper and deeper into inchoate and sometimes incoherent fantasies: images rising, spending themselves, and falling back into that sloshy darkness that conceives, spurts, and receives them back into its eternal unknown.

Two years older and a sixth grader, Janice's little knobby breasts barely rumpled her white blouse, still trying to decide when to push out and take stage, setting my mind racing with possibility. What if I could see? What would I see? When I did, what then? My imagination lunged forward, raising as much lust as a nine-year-old boy, a few years away from his first erection, could muster.

I just wanted to be around her, to touch her. Even now I'd say I felt love for her, as any puppy would love.

"H...hi...hi," I stuttered, doing my best not to meet her eyes.

"Hi." A protocol "hi," a "hi" thrown out from a place of disinterested formality, half- maybe quarter-hearted: less communication than silence would have been; a desert mirage momentarily real, spurring hope without the possibility of fulfillment.

All I could manage was a weak, nasally "Hi."

Janice walked right past me to the refrigerator, found a bottle of red pop, poured herself a full glass and sipped. That's what we called it, *red pop*: strawberry flavored, sugar saturated soda water that would fizz, shooting itty-bitty carbonated bubbles smack up into my nose right to that part of the brain that converts them into a candied delight.

Unlike the adults who gulped their drinks, Janice sipped: perhaps because of a movie she'd seen calling on her poise and presence; perhaps in rejection of her mother Irene, who, when she became drunk, which wasn't often, would swig a beer and then dribble onto her blouse, so Janice simply refused to become a clone; or perhaps because her young smallish mouth couldn't manage more.

When Janice lowered the glass her lips shone bright red. In our family, dominated by medieval terrors my grandparents brought from the farms of thirteenth century Poland—obey-or-God-will-cast-you-into-the-very-mouth-of-the-devil-where-you-will-burn-for-eternity—their threats made certain the red pop on her lips was as close as Janice, at her age, would get to wearing lipstick.

Still, to me, red pop or not, I saw lipstick: moist, risqué, rapturous lipstick.

"Come on," Irene commanded before I could say anything more, herding my mother and Janice out of the kitchen toward the living room. My mother looked back as an afterthought and nodded for me to follow, but her attention had already shifted so it didn't really matter whether I followed or not.

In the living room, what we all called the front room, larger than the kitchen by only a few square feet, a gold-green cast lit everyone's face. Gold from an incandescent table lamp shone through the thin, unfashionable lampshades, hand-me-downs passed through several families and suffering their last tour of familial obligation. Pale green reflected back from the flocked wall paper, original with the house, revealing more of its greenness than it otherwise might have, because the thread-bare fabric on the lampshades allowed easy passage from bulb to wall and back.

A couch and two arm chairs, upholstered in a shade of brown that would have remained unassuming if it hadn't become coco-mint in its surrender to the green walls, provided basic seating, especially since my family spent very little time in the front room. We lived our daily lives primarily in the kitchen, the dining room being used specifically for dining only on very special occasions.

A prized piece of furniture, a large 1946-model Philco radio-phonograph housed in a mahogany console, sat in the dining room against the wall adjacent to the archway into the front room. It served my family as a mid-20th century entertainment center and for me as an escape-way. When the door opened, the phonograph would slide out. I'd never seen a record, not a 78 or 45, until I brought the first one into the house when I turned fourteen—Bill Haley's "Rock Around the Clock"—a 45 RPM I was forced to throw into the trash because that's where my mother and father said it belonged. But I loved the radio. The shows I listened to as I curled up on the floor gripped my imagination and I would let them take me wherever they were going.

The front room was neither formal nor forbidding. We simply did not live in it. But when the family arrived for Friday night cards the evening would begin with everyone gathering in the front room and my father Ed had to set out an additional four metal folding chairs so that most of them could sit.

When my Uncle Jerry and his wife Mary Therese arrived, my mother clenched Mary Therese by the arm urging, "Come in, come in." Even though the card party gathering was a ritual most everyone enjoyed, for some the highlight of the week, and rarely did anyone miss it, my mother's grip gave the impression that she feared Mary Therese might turn around and walk back out the door. "How are you? Come in, come in."

"Just fine, Helen, just fine," Mary Therese drawled, leisurely and fluid, like she might be lounging on a veranda from *Gone With The Wind* before those wretched evil Yankees came galloping in and burned it to the ground.

But Mary Therese had not been born nor raised on a majestic, aristocratic Southern plantation. She was from Texas, a small-town girl, the daughter of a sharecropper. She wasn't Polish, but she was at least Catholic. This last part of her pedigree gained her a conditional citizenship in the family, though she always found herself at the edge—in this instance choosing a small metal folding chair tucked in a corner next to the sofa.

Plain-faced and perpetually without makeup, her fleshless lips vanishing inward, she wore her customary costume consisting of a plain housedress and her thin brown hair in a tight bun. She never drank and seemed to be consciously cultivating the character of the old biddy, not by choice, but as though somebody had to and, of all the women, she best fit the role.

"Hello Helen," her older brother Jerry said, distant and aloof.

"Hello, Jerry," my mother responded in kind, handing him the protocol bottle of Strohs.

A stiff reserve always existed between them.

Family legend had it that in his late teens Jerry impregnated a young girl which, as the story was told—but only in the most discreet and muzzled terms—brought anathema down on the girl, yet he escaped without a scratch; legally, religiously, or even to his standing in the community.

At six-feet two inches with curly brown hair and wide blue eyes, Jerry, the oldest of the five men my mother called "The Brothers," stood behind his wife. As the oldest he assumed the status of man-of-the-family—an assumption to which the others deferred but never actually agreed and mocked sometimes to his face but mostly behind his back.

"Did you guys hear about what just happened in Congress?" using his Stroh's like a conductor's baton. Jerry never just spoke. He announced. "Some woman Senator, I think she's from Maine, just made a speech about communists in the government." Silence. "You guys think there's communists in the government?"

In another day and certainly in another family Jerry's interest in politics might have led to his running for public office. But as it was all he could do was talk about politics, as those who live under the power of its authority typically do.

He imagined himself qualified to comment on national politics and elected himself as guide and teacher for the rest of the men in the family. His lack of real-world understanding never prevented him from expressing his views.

"Did you guys hear?" Silence again. "What about you Eddie? You think so?"

My father, who every one of his generation called Eddie, barely looked up. "Would communists be any different from what's in Washington now? Money's all they're about."

"Yeah...well," Jerry became animated, as though he'd been invited to continue.

"Jerry," Bo interrupted, "we're here to play cards, okay?"

"But..." Jerry tried.

"Cards, Jerry. Cards."

"Yeah...well...anyway..." If Jerry had had a meter measuring his enthusiasm, its pointer would have collapsed to near zero. He put the Strohs to his lips, held it there as he paused for a moment, weighing some thought or feeling or perhaps just the emptiness, scanned the room gauging whether or not it would be worth pushing back, decided against it, and sipped. The silence that followed was a silence that had taken up residence in and punctuated the conversations of our family: sometimes awkward, at other times painful, always familiar.

Uncle Julli and his wife Vaneta (Van), who lived next door and were the second couple to have arrived, squeezed together on the couch, a Stroh's ramrod straight-up between Julli's thighs. Van would drink occasionally but most often didn't, thinking it better to keep an eye on her husband.

The brightest and most handsome of The Brothers, Julli was a handful, and Van's stoicism, not a philosophical stance but a mix of peasant impotence and seething cynicism, served her as well as anything might.

She was the least religious of all my relatives, male or female. She did go to church for mass and baptisms but mostly to avoid community scorn. As for her belief—minimal, and devotion—none. Whenever issues of church and religion were discussed she'd roll her eyes and snort her ridicule. "Hmmphph, you actually believe that crap?"

When challenged, her expression narrowed to a cold stare as she tore into whatever point was being made.

Although I wasn't fluent in Polish I knew enough to piece together what I heard my aunts frequently ask, "Why is Van so mean?" A handy question they could puzzle over, diverting their attention from their own personal storms.

The Old Country women condemned her in private because they couldn't compete with her whip smart brain, which she used to confuse and befuddle them, and her lashing tongue that meted out mockery and disdain. Inasmuch as they couldn't outright challenge her, they merely muttered, and Van pretty much left them alone.

In isolated instances Van would scrap the 7UP in favor of a double-shot of straight Seven Crown and proceed to tie one on, freeing her brain from the ever-present, ever-powerful doppelganger who'd punish her from its fortress inside her head. If it hadn't been for family demands and community expectations she would have come out as an atheist. Instead, she'd dive with abandon into the occasional drunken release only to seal up again and live under the pressure of her own resented capitulation. Like everyone else Van had to live in the neighborhood, and for that there was a price: conformity.

During the Great Depression, Julli, at nineteen, train-hopped for six months and hoboed his way across the northern tier of the United States, begging food and doing odd jobs as he rolled through Wisconsin, Minnesota, Montana, and then down the west coast into California and back to Detroit. He treasured his "train hopping rail days" with deep pride. It had been years since he ran alongside a boxcar just beginning to roll and throw himself safely through a large door, a door that wasn't supposed to be open, landing inside on the wooden floor, hoping not to be stuck with splinters, happy to begin the next leg of his adventure. Even though twenty years had passed, he could still remember in exact succession the names of all the towns that ribboned eastward as he rolled out of Los Angeles back toward Detroit, leaving California behind to swallow the sunset.

Julli regaled the family with stories of escaping the railroad dicks whose job it was to catch the train-hoppers and send them to jail, and how seriously those dicks, with their guns and clubs, took their jobs, "They were assholes, but they had a job to do;" or the families that took him in and fed him, "I felt like a prince;" and the guys he bummed with, "Good guys. Really good guys."

However, once back in Detroit, and unable to prevent dissolving back into the family ego-mass, his "rail days" became a ruthless, unrequited longing, an acid eating away the luster from his memories, feeding the darkness that had been part of his person since boyhood.

Irene, delighting in the mists of her one Seven and Seven, a drink-you-under-the-table type she was not, floated into the front room. Her fermented buoyancy, coupled with the tickle of the irrepressible rascal who had long ago set up shop in her personality, pushed her to, as she would say, "stir the shit."

Janice had nestled-in on the floor in front of the arm chair her father Bo had selected, and as he placed his legs on either side of her and squeezed, she smiled, looked back to her father, and took another sip of red pop.

My mother took one of the metal folding chairs near the archway into the front room. My father had brought them home from a local hall the church used for bingo games. When the church pastor learned that my family held poker and pinochle evenings he gave the chairs as a gift in recognition of my mother's help at the weekly bingos where she sold bingo cards at the door when people arrived and closed the hall at the end of the night.

Passing her husband Bo, Irene waltzed from Jerry to Julli kissing them on the cheek, an unspoken but necessary ritual obeisance expected of one who was not entirely incorporated into the family.

Once the kissing was done she strutted toward my father in a mock-torrid, ungainly tango and sat on the arm of his chair.

My father's face closed down. It was his style to say very little and retain his sense of superiority, especially over The Brothers most of whom he judged to be foolish, and an even more serious indictment—incompetent.

Like Irene, my father was an outsider. His father, *dziadek* (grandfather) Louis, whom we called *dziadzia* Louie, made his living as a numbers bookie. Although almost everyone on the block placed penny, nickel, and quarter bets with Louie hoping to "hit it big," they cursed him for bringing crime to the neighborhood and for desecrating the value of work.

Louie never had to use his back in the factories. He saw himself as above physical work and, instead, took his betting ledger to the factory gates. He could work the factory gates because he paid off the city police and the private Ford Motor Company security guards. The workers knew it, but the idea of "hitting their number" was too promising for any of them to complain. They would line up to get their chance at the big win, which could mean perhaps three or four hundred dollars maximum, which in 1950 was a lot of money. But the reality of it almost always meant another hope foreclosed, another dream dashed.

The people in our neighborhood saved their coins for Louie's booking parlor, a small square niche added to the side of his backyard barn, and hid their biting scorn for him behind his back. *Dzia dzai* Louie made more money, five to ten times more, than anyone in the neighborhood, by simply collecting their change and making an occasional payout. He was as common as every other dirty fingernail in the community, yet he considered himself a person of high rank. My father, the oldest and most intelligent of his three sons, suffered from Louie's buried but crippling insecurity which often exploded into physically abusive rages.

When Louie offered the business to my father, he refused. Not from any moral compunction but because he was ashamed of his father. But even my father's shame, which everyone knew he felt, was not enough to redeem him. His outlier status, streaked with a shade of outlaw guilt-by-association, quadrupled his remoteness: distant from his family, from my mother's family, from us, and from himself.

As I grew older he shared with me some of the thoughts he kept locked away in the vault of his vigilantly kept dignity. They contained no profanity. As the target of Irene's mischief, he remained silent.

"How the f..." Irene stopped short as she saw her preadolescent eleven-year-old daughter stop mid-red-pop-sip and lean forward. Irene reconsidered, winked at the others and then turned back to him—"how the ef are you, Eddie?"

My father held seriously to his personal code of no cussing, just as he stubbornly insisted that his shoes were shined. And they were, every day, with spit and without fail. "When your shoes are shined you're a real man," he once advised me.

He heard cussing everywhere around him every day but he didn't expect or even want others to agree with his perspective. His position was more about personal presence. "It's how you come across to others that's important" he would say: peculiar for a guy who spent the majority of his time standing in the oil, grease, and metal shavings on the factory floor.

But Irene had thrown the challenge.

I watched my father stiffen, and I knew he wouldn't give an inch.

"Aw come on, Eddie, how the ef are you?" she giggled and kissed him on the cheek, much closer to his mouth than she'd kissed the other men. Not promiscuous. Suggestive. She knew my father would rather not have been kissed at all and that's exactly why she did it. Then, as she looked to my mother, she winked. "How's that Helch?"

"Ya, ya," my mother waived her off, embarrassed.

My mother couldn't look at him. As she dropped her eyes, pain fell across her face. Not the pain of a bruised heart. Rather their relationship suffered more from being mechanical than romantic. They had come to terms with their condition, settling into an unspoken contract assuring mutual amity, a peace more deadly than a heart attack—in truth, precisely an attack on the heart however much heart was present on their wedding day. God and everyone else forbid they should be seen as lovey-dovey. She suffered from the embarrassment of being exposed and from the humiliation of knowing that everyone knew how she and my father lived their marriage.

My father focused on the green flocked wall without blinking. He was a man of intense and disciplined will who could make himself do whatever he wanted. Years later, at fifty, after three and a half decades of smoking Camel cigarettes, at least two packs a day, he decided to quit. He did. Cold turkey. Done. Without the slightest complaint. But judgment and criticism also smoldered in his iron-willed lockup. He would not tolerate incompetence, what he believed to be a lack of care, and his "corrections" were usually cut with enervating contempt.

"Hey Eddie," Irene slapped him on the thigh, half way between his knee and his crotch, "why don't you kiss your wife like that?" She left her hand on his leg.

I saw my mother and father kiss twice: once at a wedding dinner reception when the guests used their silverware to clink glasses compelling them to kiss; and again at their fiftieth wedding anniversary party, a peck so brief and spare it might as well have been an accident.

My father's face flushed with anger.

"Aw look," Irene laughed, fully aware of his anger. "Eddie's shy. He's blushing. Eddie's blushing."

"Hey Irene," her husband Bo broke in. "Leave him alone."

Bo was sincere. When they were teenagers and into their early twenties, my father and the three oldest Brothers had been part of a street-wide gang: twenty-five same-aged males who lived on our block, enough to constitute a legitimate and formidable gang.

Bo had witnessed my father's explosive ferocity in many of the fights that brought the gang a terrifying reputation in our area of Southwest Detroit. My father had earned the nickname "Ketchup" because just before a fight the veins in his neck and temple would flood to a solid, ferocious red followed by an unrestrained violent eruption.

"Aw Bo," Irene whined like a little girl.

"Leave him alone, I told ya."

"I was just saying hello," Irene pleaded innocently.

"Just cut that shit out, okay?" Bo threw back another hard swallow of Stroh's and slammed the bottle down on the bleached-pine end-table, startling my mother.

Irene could be tough, and she put up with no one's crap, but for all of the women in the family, including her, there came a limit, an invisible wall beyond which they believed the unpredictable waited with blood red eyes. That wall may have been crossed, but only ever behind closed doors. In public the women just knew better.

Could this be that wall, north of which only savagery preyed? Irene wasn't sure. But the night promised pinochle and poker, and being the best poker player in the family she scanned the room until certain she had everyone's attention and then slowly, conspicuously withdrew her hand from my father's lap, squeezed off another wink in my mother's direction, raised her Seven and Seven, and snorted in as deep a voice as she could, "*Bowhn.*"

Bowhn is not a word in any dictionary. But its meaning was as clear in the family as the name Jesus Christ.

Bottoms up! Down the hatch! Not for sissies! In one swallow. God bless whiskey. What the fuck! *Bowhn!*

She waited for the others to follow.

Silence.

Not as purple and prohibitive as my father's, but palpable.

Julli picked at the label of the Stroh's between his legs. Jerry sidled over to the front door and looked out onto the street. Bo glanced at my father who stared past him. Van, Mary Therese, and my mother dropped their gaze. Janice sipped again. And Irene? She looked from one to the next as though to say "What the hell did I do?"

Maybe one of the red-eyed savages was peering in at the corner of a window. Maybe one of the nuns that taught their generation as well as mine was about to materialize with a wooden triangular ruler poised to punish saying, "Give me your knuckles." Maybe the Virgin Mary wept, tormented by how we poor humans inflict pain without really appreciating the guts being gored. Maybe...?

My mother fidgeted until she could no longer stand the benumbed wail buried deep in the familiar silence and she stood, "Anybody need another round?"

As was my habit I sat at a distance, watching, this time from a chair at the far end of the dining room, the room between the front room and the kitchen. I never fantasized about having "real" parents or different relatives like some children do. What I saw in the front room were my real parents and real relatives. I knew that. I just never felt connected. They lived in some other world. That feeling was tangible, sometimes terrifying, because I felt like a piece of wood floating on a vast body of water, unmoored, mostly unwanted. I had food, clothing, and shelter, but life in my house always seemed like it belonged to others. I was an accidental satellite, attached more by gravity than connection, more by their obligation than appreciation.

As I watched, the front room and everyone in it began to recede and become flat, one-dimensional, without perspective, and their normal size reduced as though someone had flipped binoculars and suddenly my family became midgets—far away.

This was not the first time I'd experienced a change of perspective. Sometimes the opposite happened, a room or a person would suddenly seem gigantic, bearing down on me until it was flat up against my face, and I felt like I had to struggle to prevent being sucked into another world. Other times objects moved, this way or that, and I could never be sure whether they had or hadn't. Usually I enjoyed the illusions and wondered what made them occur, but not those where I might be sucked in.

This time the flow of action in the front room froze. My mother, caught midway in her rise from the chair, stood stooped, unfinished, suspended, waiting for some force, some spark to re-animate her. Julli, Van, Jerry, Mary Therese, Bo, Janice, and Irene were fixed like mannequins in need of that same spark. Only my father moved. He turned slowly and looked directly at me.

Why hadn't he become frozen like the others? I craned my neck and arched my head toward him expecting to hear something from him, but he said nothing.

BAM. Suddenly, instantly the front room and everyone in it smashed back to normal size, moving and speaking again and I felt a slight, coolish breeze along the side of my face. The breeze wafted along in my mother's wake as she passed me on her way to the kitchen. For a split second, she seemed like a giant and I had to shake my head to reorient.

The house shuddered.

Or was it me?

Our house, about eighty years old, repeated in lock-step the design features of every other house on the block: wood frame, painted white with a gun-metal gray front porch; three floors including the basement; three small bedrooms on the first floor, mine just big enough to hold a single bed, a small chest of drawers, hooks for coats and jackets screwed into a two-by-four nailed to the wall behind the door, and on the wall behind my bed the ever-present crucifix to insure the necessary supernatural oversight to guard against what? At nine, what could I have done that needed crucifixion as a constant reminder, other than, of course, the sin of having been born human?

The living room was carpeted. All the other rooms were covered with cheap linoleum. In the bathroom, a smoky-grey shade reminded me of the film on some of the old men's teeth; and oh yes, the enclosed window-lined back porch, the only access to the back yard and basement, functioned as a repository for all manner of things—trash can, fishing rods, shoes-to-be-left-out-there-and-not-brought-in-the-house, old newspapers, and a crucifix. A crucifix hung in every room of the house save the room with the toilet out of respect for the divine.

That night the most important thing on the back porch was the *beczka*, the galvanized half-barrel, sometimes used by my mother as an extra tub on laundry day. But when everybody came over to play cards the *beczka* was filled with ice and served as a reservoir for more Stroh's.

Our house was the hub of our family life: the center from which all spokes radiated; the high court from which all family laws issued; the council before which family spats were mediated; the gathering place for minor celebrations like birthdays and all High Holidays—Christmas, Easter, and Good Friday; and an emotionally fortified residence ruled over by Anna (pronounced Ahn-na) my maternal grandmother we called *busia*, who lived in the apartment upstairs.

At nineteen she had immigrated to the New World from a religiously-fundamental farmhold in rural Poland, a closed society that viewed education as Satan's enticement to rebel and delivered little more of it than was necessary to harvest the land. America might as well have been a new universe for Anna filled with heathens, reprobates, and ne'er-do-wells, godless men who lusted for the immaculate, at least according to the impure images that mercilessly harassed her lonely imagination compelling her to cling to her faith as one would cling to a mask in the middle of a gas attack.

My mother told me that Anna had wanted to be a nun. She'd attended mass every morning for most of her life but her parents had forbidden her from entering the convent. They'd born the dead weight of their peasant's life, made heavier by the pressures of Catholic doctrine, and given that Anna was the prize of their litter, their princess, they believed she rightfully deserved a better life. And that meant...

Ah-merr-eee-ka.

I'd also heard, among the many family stories, that, religious fervor notwithstanding, she'd been attracted to a young man in Poland, *piękny* (beautiful) my mother said she called him, and was buffeted between the church and her aroused and sensual desires.

She'd left her home country to travel alone by boat with utter strangers, arriving with not one shred of English on Ellis Island, where four giant turrets of the Great Hall, a building larger than anything she'd ever imagined or seen before, towered over the dock. All of the émigrés were herded off the boat, each wearing a white identification tag on their shirts or hats, carrying everything they considered dear in dilapidated leather bags and pillow-case bundles of various sizes and shapes.

Anna lined up to wait her turn at one of the long tables in the induction center. Terror gripped her because she would have to speak, or at least attempt a response, and she wondered what punishment awaited her for her lack of English. She prayed desperately for something or someone to help her pass inspection, which, in her fear-fogged brain, loomed more like an inquisition.

Greeted by a Polish-speaking inspector she would have wept from relief had she not been so terrified by the possibility of other mistakes.

She made it through that ordeal. But, being a Catholic peasant who'd grown up in a serf's world, she focused more on her fear and never saw her success.

As she settled in Detroit, her fear never receded. Detroit visited on her much more than she could possibly have expected. To stave off the bewilderment brought on by so much that was new, she withdrew, relying on her rosary and prayer book which became more and more necessary and she became more and more isolated and desperate. Daily attendance at morning mass metamorphosed from a once-beloved celebration into a self-protective obsession. As her anxiety darkened, her soul surrendered to a sullen, shape-shifting adaptation turning her into a sour, ill-willed matriarch around whom it was very difficult to maintain any sense of aliveness or, God forbid, joy.

No doubt, in some distant recess of her bricked-over disappointment she still longed for the life of a nun. But after twelve pregnancies, including two miscarriages and one stillbirth, and her capitulation as a Catholic wife to sex—sin-soaked and indescribably vile—any hope of a holy life brought her inconsolable sorrow coupled with an ever-increasing acid rage.

Anna hovered in and over the house of my childhood as a dreadful presence.

Her husband, Antoni (pronounced Ahn-taw-knee) also came through Ellis Island. A shortish man, about five-feet-seven inches, his deference to authority ran so deep it could have been mistaken as one of the innermost rings of his family tree. Not caused by fear or weakness, at least not apparently so, his deference was the manifestation of his sincere religious conviction that authority possessed the right if not the obligation to express and impose its power and control for the well-being of everyone under its charge. If he'd picked up any rebellion-gene that might have been sprinkled through the male population of his old-country village, that piece of genetic potential had long ago burrowed into the abyssal reaches of his being, flipped a switch, and turned off the lights. His passage through the Great Hall of Induction never raised an eyebrow.

Like Anna, his destination, the city of Detroit just a few years before it burgeoned into the Motor City, had been arranged by relatives who had previously journeyed to the New World. Why Detroit? Because before cars, Detroit was an American frontrunner in the industrial age. With Vernors ginger ale, Strohs beer, Sanders candy, cake, and ice cream, all produced in mass quantities, as well as its leading industry, stove and kitchen range manufacturing, Detroit exemplified vibrancy, prosperity, future safety, and security.

Henry Ford's dominance over early twentieth-century America, and especially Detroit, had not yet emerged, although, for anyone who cared to look, he was waiting, breathlessly, in the wings.

So there they were, Antoni and Anna, both nineteen, unknown to each other, shepherded into a community of people who could at least speak their native language—an ethnic island sanctuary in the midst of a sea of other ethnic island sanctuaries—each watching the other to confirm their fear that the devil surely would be found in one of the others and not in their own.

Uprooted from what they knew and assigned by family bonds to a promise of a better life—which was difficult to see and certainly difficult to believe in—Anna continued to build the walls of what turned out to be the asylum of her inner life, while Antoni would have a few Strohs to wash down the Seagram's he drank, both of them in search of comfort and a sense of home.

But that was not to last. They had to marry. How else would they survive and contribute to fortifying their little tag end of the New World? Besides, Anna, on the eve of turning twenty, would soon become an embarrassment if not a shame if she remained without a husband and without child. Something had to be done. So the community arranged for them to meet.

I'd heard they weren't bad looking then, in an eastern European peasant sort of way. But picturing her as attractive was hard for me because when I knew her she wore plain usually grey house dresses with sleeves to her elbows, a hem at mid-calf, wrapped in a plain work-a-day apron. When, as a Christmas gift, my mother bought her a house dress in a red and blue floral pattern with white lace at the collar she rejected it as vulgar and whorish. "*Wystd!* Feh!"

Even as a young woman she wore plain dresses to church with her ever-present babushka, the signature headscarf that tied below the chin, the headdress of a reverent Catholic woman and a badge of the people of the land. There was no land in Detroit, or at least none that meant anything to this cluster of Poles, but that made little difference. A babushka was part of her standard costume. What could she have been expected to wear: a large, wide-brimmed hat with a glorious feather, cocked to one side for strutting her stuff on the boulevard? She had no stuff to strut, at least none that she believed in or cared about and the streets of her neighborhood, more like lanes, would permit just two horse-drawn wagons to pass and then two cars when they entered the scene.

At first Antoni picked up odd jobs, trading his back for a few dollars, and his daily gear reflected his station—bib overalls, denim shirts, and work boots. His luck changed when Ford's ascendancy infused the local zeitgeist, calling men, many, many men to help the assembly-line Pharaoh build his New World kingdom. Antoni was one of those men, landing a job in one of Ford's foundries where he stayed.

Antoni and Anna met at an afternoon backyard party given to celebrate someone's old-country style baptism. They both knew they were there to meet each other and so they arrived with the proper amount of decency for her and courtesy for him. To avoid scandal, marriage was a must. At their age they couldn't wait much longer without bringing down a rain of scowling gossip and alienation within their community.

When they were brought face-to-face, the moment strained politeness. Anna couldn't keep the image of the beautiful young man in Poland from invading her mind and Antoni was no match. And to her disgust, which all of her will could not prevent from registering on her face, the thought of making babies with Antoni, which was the point of marriage, caused her to silently recite the Our Father and the Hail Mary to protect her immortal soul from the repulsive thoughts she could not control.

Back in Poland Antoni had had the reputation of someone who could *przelecieć panienkę*, bed the ladies. He wasn't beautiful. Simply typical. But he was aggressive and determined. He loved most seducing or coercing his lays out in the open fields and then he could tell his friends, "My ass was bumpin' in the wind."

But now there she stood in a red and blue floral housedress, a party dress, with white lace at the collar and her babushka tightly tied. He'd plunged into babushka-headed women before and loved to hear them howl, but something about Anna, that she looked either angry or not feeling well, he couldn't tell for certain, caused him to think about a shot and a beer.

It was hoped, of course, they would like each other. But no matter, marriage was the point.

After the party when Anna was asked what she thought, she felt something she'd only ever felt once before when her father would not permit her to enter the convent. She felt a sense of collapse, of hopelessness and resignation. And when asked again what she thought she said, *Wszystko będzie dobrze* (It will be okay).

The Polish community knew of Antoni's "bedding" prowess and wanted him married off. And within the community Anna was the only female of eligible age. They were a perfect couple.

So Antoni the wolfhound and Anna, stoic and enduring, married. His job was to have a job. Hers was to have children. He worked in the factory. She became a factory.

"Hellooo," Uncle Ari sang out from between our house and Uncle Julli's house next door. It was his custom to tap his arrival on every window along the side of our house beginning with the one in the front room.

Five years my mother's junior, Ari was the heart of the family, kind, loving, and generous. As an infant, his sweetness captured everyone's attention and affection, most especially my mother's.

Their generation, the first born in the United States, created their own semantic recipes, tossing Polish and English into their own particular word-mush to make wrestling with a two-language world as manageable as they could.

For example, the Polish phrase, *Dziecci grają na ulicy*, translates to "children play in the street." My relatives massaged and mangled it into '*dziecci playovatch na streetciech*.' The "*ovatch*" rode tail to the English word "play" creating a kind of hybrid, while "street" was bedecked with "*ciech*," both forms assuring the first-arrivers that those born in the New World had absolutely not abandoned their roots. This linguistic amalgam, this Engpolsh, served to assist those born in Detroit to communicate with each other and with those from the Old Country—sometimes surprisingly well and sometimes not at all.

"*Jest kto w domu?* Anybooddddy hommmme?" Uncle Ari sang out, his joyous voice reverberated between the houses setting the sound waves themselves to giggling. Uncle Ari was the only one who could get away with a little joy as Anna's shadow walked unflagging patrol along the verges between spontaneity and sin.

His hey-I'm-here serenades, like the cries of a homing pigeon within the last few flaps of returning to the coop, were the personal stamp that set him apart from his brothers. Like his brothers, however, Ari was locked in to the magnetic fields generated by Seven Crown and pinochle, and he followed the siren call of his family, an irrepressible though inscrutable yearning that drew him home time and again.

At the sound of his voice I jumped from my chair, thrilled, positioning myself in the kitchen to be sure he would see me when he came in. Uncle Ari had always been my favorite: the only one of The Brothers who listened to me with care and curiosity. I felt good around him. Ari actually enjoyed showing affection. He did with me and I gave it back.

My mother, who'd already stationed herself at the sink/bar to get away from Irene's "funny business" with my father, uncapped a Strohs, filled a shot glass to its lip with Seven Crown and waited, beaming a smile. She loved Ari most. He was the second youngest of The Brothers whom my mother had been assigned responsibility for raising. So he viewed her as his mother.

Before Ari could make it through the back door, Julli flew in from the front room, his alcoholic version of the homing pigeon, knowing another round was being poured.

"Hellooo!" he mimicked Ari. Julli always mimicked whomever was getting attention, hungry for what he could not get on his own.

My mother neither laughed nor smiled.

"Pour me one too, Helch." For Julli that "too" gave him permission to ask for another shot because the others would.

"Julli," my mother frowned, her voice dark and forbidding, stretching out his name as a sign of her disapproval.

There were nights when Julli, unlike the homing pigeon, could not find his way home. Locked into his own set of magnetic lines composed of a blend of corn, rye, barley, yeast, and water, aged in the tensions of his barrel chest, fermenting current and ancient hurts into a bitterness flavored with disillusionment and defeat, distilled down to the victim's cry—"It's not my fault"—Julli flew a route that added a predilection for meanness to the cruel shade of red that was his nose.

"What?" His black eyes flared, reflecting the light from the five-and-dime milk-glass fixture on the ceiling.

She continued to stare, her eyes filling with the pain of loving this man whose 80-proof insulation had almost completely sealed him off.

"What?" he barked again.

"You know." She turned away. "You know."

"Oh Helch, just one more. Ari's here." My mother relented, pouring him another belt of Seven Crown that he held up toward the door anticipating Ari's entrance.

Ari tapped on the kitchen window.

Without looking to my mother, Julli whispered, "It's okay, Helch. It's okay."

My mother knew how Julli struggled with the family, the neighborhood, with whiskey, and with himself, but she had no idea what to do about it. None. She wasn't an unintelligent woman but woefully inexperienced and thoughtlessly naïve. She had only one source she could draw upon: her past hopelessly circumscribed by superstition and Catholic dogma, placing the cause of Julli's alcoholism on the vicious deceptions of the devil, a belief which imposed the burden of guilt and humiliation for being weak. For my mother a good honest confession seemed the only possible cure.

"I know, Julli," she softened, her body slumping in affectionate resignation, "I know."

"Hellooo." The door thrust open, and, like a seasoned actor, Ari posed for a moment in the jamb, smiling like Santa Claus.

"*Jak tam, wsczyscy?* How's everyone?" His affection for his family radiated like a crisp full moon. "*Jak tam?*"

He too spoke Engpolsh. "*Yak tam*" literally means "as there." But in Engpolsh it acquired a rich dimensionality carrying the ideas—"How's everybody?" or "How's it going?" or "What's happening?" or "I'm here." or "What's new?" or whatever you wanted it to mean as long as it was a greeting.

I ran to him, wrapped my arms around his waist, flattened my face into his heart space, and squealed, "Uncle Ari! Uncle Ari!"

"Hellooo," he hugged, tossing me back and forth in the circle of his arms. "Jimush, Jimush," he sang out through his puckish smile while rubbing the top of my head, "Where'd you get all these curls?"

"Shhhh," my mother admonished.

Any mention of my curls chafed at a sore spot between my mother and me. Although natural, as confirmed in the three photographs taken of me when I was an infant, which she had made a point to show me, I resented my curls and blamed her because of what she did one evening when I was in kindergarten.

Our exclusively Polish parish—identified by the name of our church, Our Lady Queen of Angels, the centerpiece of our community—covered an area ten blocks square. Queen of Angels supported an elementary school to which parents were obligated, under the pain of social denunciation, to send their children, and which celebrated five and six-year-olds who completed kindergarten with a formal ceremony—Graduation to First Grade. Most of the neighborhood attended: immediate family, extended family, church members, even strangers. Anyone considered a stranger had either just moved in and hadn't passed surveillance, or was a blood relative of an insider, or was just passing through. The last were watched carefully.

The people of Queen of Angels were poor, but not poverty stricken. They worked hard keeping the area spic-and-span: lawns, sidewalks, curbs, streets, even alleyways behind their houses. "You could eat off the streets," the women said proudly. "Queen of Angles ain't no nigger town."

Even though Catholic and devout, bigotry spewed from their lips like second-nature, the paradox of innocence and intolerance. Blacks and Jews made up their primary targets. But they were not averse to including their own people as objects of callous discrimination. After the Second World War when Polish refugees from Eastern Europe immigrated to Detroit, the people of Queen of Angels called them DPs, "displaced persons," and they did so with the same careless malice they directed toward those they called niggers and kikes.

Despite their Old Country aversion to education, their growing appreciation and respect for kindergarten graduation evidenced a turning toward New World attitudes and values. But saddled by their Old Country identification with hard physical work, the boys of my parents' generation were likely to leave school before finishing the eighth grade to later end up in a factory. The girls continued on and some, though not many, even achieved a high school diploma. It was collectively and silently understood that the girls were kept in school to keep them out of...well...you know..."trouble."

My father was an exception. At fourteen, after staunching and at times brutal encouragement by one of his uncles, he applied and was accepted to Henry Ford trade school. Even though he hated school, he possessed a natural talent for mechanics and flourished. His peers, those who did not resent him for his success, considered him well educated.

"Henry Ford," he would later say, "was the reason I kept a job during the Depression:" the only man on our block who did.

I had been chosen valedictorian for my kindergarten graduation and had to deliver the welcoming address for the ceremony which sent my mother into a fit of ecstasy: not because I'd been acknowledged, but because of what she could say at the corner market, to women on the street, and at any of her many church events. "My Jimush is valedictorian," a word whose meaning she didn't fully grasp, and certainly not the implications, and whose pronunciation gave her a hard and somewhat embarrassing time. "He's speaking for the graduation."

Speaking? I was five! Years later, in her sixties, she confessed, "If I could've gone back to school I would've studied public speaking."

She also told me that she loved me deeply when I was an infant and totally dependent. However, as I began to grow, as I began to assert myself, she became confused and frightened. Even though she raised Ari and Chez almost single-handedly, she said, "I just never knew what to do with you."

But I was just five, and she was determined that I look "Just so." So she forced me to sit still as she curled my hair with a wooden-handled two-prong, metal curling iron she heated in the blue flame flickering from one of the burners on the gas stove in the kitchen.

Did I scream? Yes. Did I twist and squirm? Yes. Did I beg? Yes. Did it matter? No.

Six grotesque curls on the very top of my head, each the size of a silver dollar, accompanied me to my graduation ceremony and displayed my shame and impotence for all to see, and especially for me to bear. And to add additional insult, they were called "sausage curls."

"*Co to jest?*" (What's this?) Anna snorted when she saw my hair. "Sausage head," she chastised, and, in an occurrence as rare as public affection between Antoni and Anna, she supported me—against my mother.

"I love curly hair," Ari bellowed, as though his volume alone would repair the breach between my mother and me. He placed my face between his hands, large enough to make my cheeks disappear, "Jimush, Jimush, see my hair. Straight, brown, not curly like yours. I wish I had your…"

"*Bowhn*," Julli broke in snapping Ari's attention away from me. "What the hell are you doing? It's time to drink." Julli didn't care about my feelings or my mother's. He just wanted the Seven Crown and believed he would be partially forgiven if Ari drank too.

Ari looked to my mother, back to Julli, then back to me, his love of family peace in a two-out-of-three limbic match with his love of a good party…until…"Where's mine, Helch?"

"That's better," Julli smiled.

I hated him for pulling Uncle Ari away.

My mother moved toward Ari carefully, shot glass in hand, making certain not a drop would spill: a way for her to say "I love you."

Ari took and raised his glass to his older brother in a gesture of affection and respect, "*Bowhn*, brother Julli."

Their heads snapped in unison like a precision drill team who'd practiced since Ari was a teenager, propelling the Seven Crown to the back of their throats.

"Hey Jesuuus, that's good," Ari laughed as though the flavor surprised him, a flavor he'd tasted countless times before. All of the men actually liked the taste of Seven Crown which amazed me.

"Ari, let us in," his wife Blanche whined.

Still in the doorway, his entrance more important than his wife behind him, he had blocked her from coming in.

He hadn't forgotten her. Ari loved Blanche far more than any of the other Brothers or my father loved or even imagined loving their wives. But once he launched a riff, and especially one that delighted him, like any good performer—the show's the thing.

Uncle Ari turned sideways in the doorway, raised his arms pretending to be a draw-bridge, flashed his eyes at Julli, and pushed himself flush against the frame making just enough room for Blanche to enter.

"For God's sake, Ari!" She tried to push through, shoulders squared and thrown back, unwilling to adjust to his crowding the doorway. Just as she was mid-way through Ari puffed out his chest and pinned her to the opposite frame. "We haven't even got here yet and you've already had one." She forced a smile to cover her irritation and to show my mother and Julli that she was only teasing.

Ari dropped his head feigning contrition. "I know, honey. I can't help it."

As Blanche tried again to push through, Ari pinched her on the butt. She screamed and swatted his hand, her smile shifting into a serrated giggle.

It wasn't the pinch she resented, although when she complained to some of the other women they counseled, "At least he still grabs your ass." They didn't understand that it was his irrepressible playfulness in public she couldn't abide because she thought it unmanly.

"*Jak tam*, Blanka," (Polish for Blanche) my mother broke in.

"Helcha you know how your brother is." Blanche shook her head covering her annoyance with a roll of her eyes. "He never listens. I tell him and tell him, but..."

Ari hugged her from behind, "I'm sorry, Blanche."

"Oh sure he is," she protested as she worked to keep the bubble in her voice from fading. "I don't know what I'm going to do with him."

"I do," Ari whispered as he stroked her fleshy rump.

"*Wystd*," my mother spun to the sink/bar to get Ari his chaser—the inevitable Strohs. "Shame."

Unable to contain herself, Blanche's façade burst, "God damn it, Ari..."

Julli grabbed the uncapped Strohs from my mother, handed it to Ari, clinked it with his own, "Here's to," and they both enjoyed a long, cold swig.

"Hey, what the hell we gotta do, wait here all night?" Uncle Czeslaw shouted, standing in the doorway, squinting one eye to ward off the smoke wafting up from the Lucky Strike drooping from his lips.

An irremediable chain smoker Czeslaw, whom everybody called Chez, would very often light a new cigarette with the still hot end of the one he was about to crush in the ashtray, but before he did he would take the last few drags to be sure he got everything the dying cigarette had to offer. The skin of his fore and middle fingers on his right hand had long ago turned yellow-brown from the smoke that curled around and dug deep into his skin, wrapping around his fingers like an addict's tattoo.

Having arrived with Ari and Blanche, Chez and his wife Violet stood in the doorway.

Ari and Chez had been inseparable from Chez's birth. Chez, who possessed his own eye-twinkle though not quite up to Ari's, was eleven months Ari's junior. Chez did not defer but often, and with respect, played second-fiddle to Ari's lead. Most times they traded playing straight-man to each other's joker.

Chez enjoyed and respected the show Ari had been putting on in the kitchen and waited, making sure not to interfere.

Anna and Antoni had bred two different families. The first consisted of Jerry, Julli, Bo, and my mother—the "first-family" children. My grandparents needed to create a foothold in the New World and what better way than by begetting their own brood, their own personal buffer and protection? What better way to insure their own survival, to assure they had caretakers for their old age?

While Anna and Antoni were *in* the New World they were certainly never *of* it. Anna never learned English and Antoni managed just enough to get along.

Instead Anna created her own inner reality built on the memories which took her back to her little village church and the crucifix above the altar she so adored. Her Detroit existence extended only as far as the Queen of Angels church building, a direct five-block walk, and whomever she met along the way. Otherwise, her house and the street on which it stood circumscribed her every day. Beyond that she rarely ventured and then only with my mother or one of the boys.

Antoni, small framed yet very strong, made their livelihood in the hot and filthy Ford foundry. He dreamt of the farms back in Poland—green, breezy, as high as the sky—a far cry from the grease stained machinery silhouetted against the red-hot glow of his confined and restrictive workplace. And he reminisced with his immigrant buddies at a local tavern. "How did I end up in this hell?" he'd ask and they would just shrug their shoulders. "Who the fuck knows?" he'd answer his own question and throw back another shot.

Anyway, what did it matter? In the New World of factories men left the house and went off to work because that's what men did.

As the family grew, the first four children, as part of their birth obligation, bore the responsibility of succession, of assuring that the family would actually take root and thrive in America. They were the ones to prove the promise that a better life could be and would be realized.

Anna ruled the house with a strap and her own dread-filled catechism. Fierce and forbidding she drew her children into her own unnerved world, a world of demons that had to be subdued to keep one's soul from corrupting. There was no time to play. Like on the farms of her youth a person's value was cinched to what he or she could produce. Life meant work. Work assured life. A simple rule the first-family children learned from the time they were able.

Work stripped them of their childhood. Responsibility foreclosed on their dreams. The future? Set and settled. One consolation though—Strohs and Seven Crown.

Anna and Antoni's second family began with the birth of Ari and then Chez. By that time the cultural buffer had been established between the Old and New World anchoring Poland in Detroit and Detroit in the family. Their buffer stood safeguard against ethnic invisibility, easing Anna's anxieties, subduing some of her demons, lessening the threat of change, tranquilizing the pain of having left her homeland, consigning her hopeless longings for return to Poland to the nether reaches of her mind where they remained alive and only somewhat abusive.

The obligations the first-family lived under had softened, permitting Ari and Chez the freedom of more playfulness and fun. And by the time of their arrival my mother had grown old enough so that Anna could delegate mothering duties for them to her. For my mother, another obligation. For Anna, a release from the bondage of motherhood, a choice she confessed to my mother years later.

Chez's wife Violet, Vi we called her, did not come from roots that reached back to Eastern Europe. Nor did she exude the peasant's bouquet—a blend of liver, fried onions, cigarette smoke, and alcohol. Everybody said she brought class to the family.

Her salient feature, a pair of enormous breasts—not by comparison to the other women, but on their own, enormous—were harnessed by her special brassieres that presented her two calling cards well in advance of the rest of her. Her breasts, sculpted to stiletto points, always made me wonder: nothing like how Janice's shy nubs touched something in my belly, something hot and otherworldly. My interest in Vi's set was more mechanical. Comparing them to my own nipples,—I was too young to understand the sexual intent behind brassiere or lingerie design—I wondered if hers really did come to pencil-point tips like they always seemed to.

Also, Vi always wore cashmere sweaters; V-necked, scoop-necked, or turtle-necked. Her sweaters clung close, sliding down to her nipple points, following the round curve of the underside, and down to her flat belly. She was the Marilyn Monroe of our family.

When the family women talked about Vi they would say, "She's got real class." Quite a tribute from a family who could use *Wstyd* (shame) as a substitute for "hello."

"Hey Chez," Julli shouted, his volume dependably upsurging as more brothers gathered, "you ready for one?"

"JULLI," Van snapped, startling everyone and quieting the kitchen.

For several minutes Van had been in the dining room, just outside the kitchen, watching. She had the disquieting gift of being ghostlike. At the center of a crowded room she could go unnoticed until she spoke, invariably surprising everyone around her, and astonishing even those next to her. As soon as she'd heard Ari's window tapping she knew what to expect and began to move in the direction of limiting Julli's intake.

Julli and Van were a matched pair. Their respective species of rage fit like puzzle pieces out of which emerged their marriage: always gloomy, sometimes grim, and occasionally grisly. No one knew if any physical violence ever occurred behind closed doors but people suspected.

"What, momma? What?" Julli wailed mock-innocence to counter-punch Van's patrol-guard superiority.

Julli stood six feet tall, weighed two-hundred plus pounds, and could easily dead-lift any of his brothers from a squat. But when Van barked, the marrow sloshed in his bones. He could have killed her with one blow, but when it came to drinking she had the upper hand—at least up to a certain point beyond which there was no telling.

I think you've had enough." She didn't speak much even when she felt what most people would call 'happy.' But when she did speak she always came across as issuing a command. She rarely asked. She told everyone, even my mother and my aunts.

"What!?" Julli suddenly turned fierce.

Van's back stiffened.

"God damn it, Van, *Ja tylko miał dwa.*" When Julli reverted to Polish he was defending against collapse. "I only had two." He was teetering. Everyone knew it. Most especially Van. But like with a cornered animal there was no guarantee what he might do next.

Her jaw tightened. If she could have she would have drilled her heels into the linoleum.

"Aw, Van," Ari pulled her to him with one arm and kissed her on the forehead. "Julli's a big boy. Look at him."

"Yeah, Van," Chez added his back-up from across the room. "Look at him for cripes sake."

Julli puffed his chest, sucked in his gut, and flexed his arms in the clichéd weightlifter's pose. "See, momma. See how big I am." His attempts at comedy were painfully embarrassing.

My mother had already filled three shot glasses that Julli whisked from atop the sink/bar, keeping one and giving the other two to Ari and Chez. They all downed them before anyone could object.

"God damn it, that's really good." Julli smiled, re-assuming his pose for Van.

"Stop, Julli." Blanche pulled down his arms. She wanted to be forceful but all she could get out was a puny wail. "You're such a baby."

"Do you hear that, momma? Blanka thinks I'm a baby."

Van glared at Ari, then Chez, then finally at my mother, and turned back toward the living room.

"Geez boys," Vi crossed to the sink/bar and made a Seven and Seven. "This is supposed to be a party."

Vi's accent did not match the family's. She added syllables. For Tuesday, she would say *Tee-yews-day* instead of *Toos-day* like the others. Three syllables not two. For *have* she would say *hee-ave*. Two not one. People accused her of "putting on the dog," but no one knew for sure, including Chez. He never brought it up with her. He'd say, "That's just Vi."

"Yes, yes," my mother squeaked, tension pushing her voice up into her falsetto. "This is a party. Enough in the kitchen. Everybody to the front room."

My mother, stretched on tenterhooks between an inbred obligation to attend to her family and her deeply concealed preference to be alone, away from having to deal with people at all, secretly wished they would all just go home. But the party was on and they wouldn't.

The men filed into the front room and the women followed. Vi turned back to my mother with her stiletto breasts in high pique. "Don't give Julli so many."

"I didn't," my mother blurted. "You saw. He took them."

"Yes," Vi pointed, her finger following the line of her already accusatory breasts. "But you poured."

My mother was stunned. Caught. "What would you want me to do?"

"Just watch what you give him, okay. Just watch." Seeing the others in the front room, she smiled and left my mother scolded.

Because it wasn't Vi's style to scold, at least not publicly, my mother wondered what might be going on she didn't know about. She stood, motionless; her brow furrows growing dark, regressing deep into her skin, as though trying to recapture an innocence they could only vaguely remember.

Coldcocked by Vi into a familiar bewilderment, she reached for the small gold cross hanging from her neck. She appeared to be focused outward but her gaze turned burningly inward as she sputtered, "I couldn't say no, could I?"

Of course she couldn't say no. Not to The Brothers. Who would expect that of her?

I said nothing. My mother's dark, afflicted confusion scared me. My out-of-control knees jerked in and out catching my mother's attention.

"What?" she snarled.

"What did I do?" I yelped.

"Just do as I say."

She squeezed my shirt between her thumb and index finger and pulled me from my chair. That required little because I'd already decided to stand. Even angry, the best she could do as a show of strength was to use her thumb and index finger.

Pinochle and Poker

The front room was abuzz with the family chattering away in a mishmash of English, Polish, and Engpolsh. My father would speak only English. His resented his father with such vehemence that he rejected speaking Polish altogether to sever, as completely as he could, his connection with Louie.

Of the women, Vi's Polish was fragmented, halting and replete with grammatical and pronunciation mistakes. Even though gaffs like hers, and she made them regularly, would have been held against anyone else, she was so delightful and charming when she tried to speak Polish that no one, especially Anna, held it against her. With Anna's imprimatur, the way had been opened for Vi to pass the tests of acceptance into our family.

The conversation in the living room had, as usual, turned into a crosstalk with the men focusing on their interests as the women did on theirs. I never understood how they could hear one another, because they weren't seated women on one side and men on the other. They spread out, all cross talking simultaneously. The women spoke of each other, children, and Our Lady Queen of Angels church. The men spoke of work, cars, and the Detroit Tigers.

It's supposed to be a truism in baseball that to win a pennant a team must divide its season into thirds. They're likely to lose one-third of their games so they must win two-thirds for a championship season. In July 1950 the Tigers, having won sixty-five percent of their games, were chasing the hated New York Yankees, hated by my family with more lethal passion than they hated the dreaded Russian Communists. The men were gripped with a violent hope that the Tigers would crush the Yankees who they were playing that very night, so the radio was sure to be on in the basement. I could hear Detroit player names rise up out of the front room din: Dizzy Trout, Virgil Trucks, George Kell, and Hoot Evers. For the entire city, the Tigers had reached an almost divine status.

The divine was also well represented by the women when they talked about Our Lady Queen of Angels school and church. Our Franciscan pastor, Father Paul, using fund-raising drives in combination with his serious diocesan political skills, had announced during the ten-o'clock high mass the previous Sunday that the archdiocese of Detroit had given the green light to build a new church starting the next year. The old facility, a four-story red brick rectangle, housed the elementary school on the first two floors, a storage attic on the third, and the church in the basement. If it hadn't been for the narrow windows at the church ceiling the nave would have been largely dark.

Originally built in 1915, the fact that the church was in the basement had evidently been of no concern. But by 1950 loyal and devoted parishioners felt that no church should be underground, except for the church of the early martyrs. Our church was seen as underfoot, specifically the feet of school children and nuns on the first floor above, and parishioners took that as a sign of disrespect to the Virgin Mary. So they threw themselves wholeheartedly into raising the money however they could to correct the mistakes of their elders. That their passion was framed within the idea of correcting elders was itself stunning, because elders, especially parents and grandparents, were always to be respected—no matter what.

The new building was to be gothic and grand with a real choir loft and stained glass windows starting just above head height and reaching upward for two stories. Parishioners, in competition with nearby parishes—Saint John the Baptist, Saint Stephen, Saint Francis, Saint Hedwig, and Saint Cunegunda—couldn't wait for the new building to be completed. The others would only be churches. Our Lady Queen of Angels would be a cathedral.

"Hey, enough with the gab," Ari smiled, raising his Strohs high, "we're here for pinochle not talk. Get off your *dupas, psia krew.*" Ari laughed. "It's time to play."

I couldn't speak much Polish but I had a better understanding than my parents realized. My relatives always shifted into Polish when they were cussing, but their tone and delivery made the forbidden words obvious.

Psia krew (*pshia kreff*) and *dupa* were just a few of the many Polish cuss words that were used in my family. *Dupa* meant "ass" and *psia krew* translated into "dog's blood." I knew what *psia kreff* meant literally, but as a curse term it didn't make sense. During a birthday party in our basement, I had asked, speaking only the cuss words in Polish, how dog's blood became a cuss word. My uncles and aunts looked toward each other perplexed. They had no idea. Not one of them would even attempt an explanation.

They turned to *busia* Anna who had sequestered herself in a corner waiting for birthday cake and red pop and asked her for an explanation. Although she had announced she was not *of* the world, she dearly loved red pop, and that was enough to get her into the basement, but not much past the moment when she'd had several glasses. With her red mustache glistening, she'd take herself back up to her second floor apartment refuge from the world.

Hearing the words her immediate scowl drew down her brows so forcefully that an audible throaty gasp sucked the air out of the room followed by collective breath-holding because we knew we had ventured into profane and godless territory.

It wasn't clear whether her fierce look stemmed from what we were saying or because she had been snared by a rope made of profanity, drawing her out of her detachment and into the question at hand. Whatever the case, she was compelled to save us, and herself, and she relied on just her look buttressed by three words that ripped through us all like the voice of a condemning martyr.

"*Wstyd*" (shame).

And then, "*Nie wolno*" (It is not allowed).

She then launched a saliva-less spit toward the center of the group.

Those three words defined Anna's character. She lived in her world of *nie wolno* and directed her refusal at almost every wish, hope, or request except for those that Antoni made. As his wife, she was required to accept, though most often suffering the very *wstyd* she so abhorred in others.

"Let's go, let's go," Chez chimed in to support Ari, sweeping his nicotine-stained hand in an arc that covered the entire front room, "it's time for pinochle."

Suddenly the front room shape-shifted into what appeared to be disorganized action, but everybody knew where they were going and what to do so chaos soon blossomed, revealing its underlying order.

The men passed through the dining room on their way to the basement. The women brought the metal folding chairs and several wooden kitchen chairs to the dining room table. Although a formal mahogany table with leaves that, when set in place, enlarged it to accommodate more people, it had no chairs of its own.

I once overheard my mother and father bicker over buying chairs. "Wherever we go," she complained, "people have dining room chairs. What do we have? *Te stary drewniane rzeczy* (These wretched old things)."

"What about the folding chairs?" my father argued, defending the chairs he'd brought home from the bingo hall. "They were a gift from the priest."

"To *nie są prawdziwe* dining room chairs."

"What do you mean not genuine chairs? What genuine?"

"Wooden. Straight back. Shiny. Upholstered. Dining room chairs. Chairs I can be proud of."

Stung, my father shot back, "So put pillows on the kitchen chairs."

She stared at him as though he were some ignorant alien and muttered, "*Jestes jak Rusek*, like a Russian you are."

The women placed the motley chairs around the table and I brought out the yellow-flowered oil cloth cover from the dining room closet. My mother and Irene grabbed it from me and spread it out to protect against spillage.

Irene drew an ashtray from a stack on top of the radiator in the corner and set it beside her seat at the table. She was the only woman who smoked publicly.

I knew my mother smoked. She'd steal away into the basement and use the enclosed toilet cubicle as a hideaway. The walls of the stall didn't extend to the ceiling or the floor so anyone could see her shoes and smell the smoke.

I tried to imagine what she looked like with her underwear at her ankles, reading the paper, a cigarette hanging from her lips. All I needed was to zero in on her mouth and I could easily see smoke being sucked in and blown out. But those few times when her whole smoking face burst into my consciousness the image sent shivers of revulsion through me. "Not my mother."

The women played poker mostly for pleasure, nickel or dime ante and no bet more than a quarter. After a full evening of playing, which could last three or four hours, the big winner might go home with ten, maybe fifteen dollars more than she had when she sat down.

Only Irene believed herself to be a serious player, and the others were wary of her aggression.

"She's so cutthroat," Blanche complained, but never to Irene's face. "Sometimes it's no fun playing with her."

"I know, I know," Mary Therese offered her tepid support, the Texan in her squeezing out through her oblong-voweled drawl.

What did Jerry ever see in her?—a question that when asked among the family always gave the impression that whoever was asking wanted both to know the answer and simultaneously would have preferred that Jerry had never brought her to Detroit so the question would never have come up. As it was, he did and they really wanted to know, their damp and clammy squeamishness notwithstanding.

There were moments, fragile at best, when Mary Therese rose to an incomplete anger, an anger that frightened her more than whatever affront had called it forth. In those moments, she'd take a lace-fringed hankie from her purse, which she was never without, and dab her nose, punctiliously, as though she was trying to recapture the delicacy that once was the Old South.

The women sat, their Seven and Sevens within easy reach. Van chose to deal first, selecting a deck from three options on the table that were set out for the evening and removing the double-wrapped red rubber band that held it together. Irene lit a cigarette.

"Oh, Irene," Vi moaned.

"What?" Irene blinked, smoke curling up into her eye.

"You know what," more of a plea than a demand.

"No one's telling you to smoke." Irene routinely argued that if she died because of smoking that was her business.

"I don't care if you smoke. You know that. But when I leave my sweaters smell like smoke and I can't stand that."

"What're you talking about, sweaters?"

"They smell."

"You never talked about sweaters before," Irene pressed.

"I know," Vi shrugged apologetically. "I didn't want to make a fuss."

"For Christ sake, Vi, Chez never stops with his Luckies."

"Oh Irene," Vi's hurt was obvious. "I'm married to Chez. I love Chez. He never smokes around me."

Van shuffled. Blanche and Mary Therese withdrew into themselves intent on ducking the crossfire.

"What?" Irene, completely surprised, coughed.

"Uh huh," as if Vi had just revealed a sweet secret.

"How about when you're at home?" Irene snapped.

"In the winter, he smokes in the basement. In the summer, he's outside."

"Holy shit," Irene squawked.

"Really?" my mother blurted, blatantly surprised. "He never does that when he's here."

"You're shitting us?" Irene prodded.

"No. I'm not. He knows how I feel about cigarette smoke."

"More like how you feel about your sweaters," Blanche added.

Vi smiled.

"We all admire Vi's sweaters, Irene," my mother added. "You know that."

Irene shot her a look as though to say, 'Who let you in here?' Irene had to gather her thoughts. That Chez never smoked in Vi's presence was stunning. "He smokes when he's here," she argued.

"I know. I told him I don't mind. He's with his brothers... you know."

"What about your sweaters then?" Irene's anger became obvious, as though she'd somehow been betrayed.

"He buys me a new one."

"A new one," Van blurted.

"Uh huh."

The tension at the table had them all by their throats. Chez bought her sweaters, cashmere sweaters. Where was he getting the money? An intimacy between Chez and Vi had been exposed. Having Chez's kindness thrust into the room upset their routine. His was a tenderness best kept behind doors, an affection the others only hoped for, arousing an envy that stung like whiskey.

Vi blinked, unaware that her simple secret reverberated like the waves of an earthquake through the family routine. No one knew what to do.

"Okay, Irene?" Vi asked.

"What?" Vi's question forced Irene out of her own thoughts.

"Do you mind?"

Even though they'd all met around our table many times, they were on new ground. And what was the best move to invoke the reliable? Do what they'd always done.

"Let's play," Irene directed.

"Irene, do you mind?"

"About what?"

"Not smoking."

"Oh, yah, okay, okay," Irene rolled her eyes as though complying was no big deal and crushed her cigarette in the ashtray.

"Thanks, honey," Vi smiled. "I'd do the same for you."

Everyone was permitted to breathe again.

Van riffled through the deck and announced, "Seven card stud, red sevens and one-eyed jacks wild."

"Oh for shits sake, Van, will you call a real game?" Irene groused, sitting among what she considered amateurs.

"We always play dealer's choice, Irene, and I'm the dealer. You get to call whatever you want when it's your deal. For this hand it's seven card stud, red sevens and one-eyed jacks wild."

Irene and Van, married six months apart, had been bridesmaids for each other's weddings. They were tethered together like twins, born of the same yen for the heretical, delighting in the role of provocateur. Both instigators—Irene playful and naughty and Van piercing and combative—they would go after each other, initially competitive but affable, until their styles began to scramble each other's nerves. Once their needling turned sour, an unconcealed hostility emerged between them: example, seven card stud, red sevens and one-eyed jacks wild.

When the way Van and Irene treated each other came up in conversation—they were not present, of course—my mother would say, "*Tsk, tsk, tsk*, I'm telling you familiarity breeds contempt!" Her disdain, leavened with anger, would flare because she considered their bickering estrangement gratuitous and wasteful, and mostly because their "pissing match," as she called it, threatened family harmony. She was correct. Their skirmishing had become inane: pointless potshots for no other purpose than to irk and pester. Still, for all that, she envied them; not their jousting which she could never have survived because she didn't have the wit nor the will to keep up with the back-and-forth. They had a deep connection that led her to sometimes say, "It's better than nothing."

"Everybody in?" Van counted the coins at the center of the table and started to deal.

I knew only the rudiments of poker, enough to play but not enough to win. I didn't have a killer instinct, so neither winning nor losing really mattered. The thought of sitting at a table for three hours with the intent of defeating the others so that I could take their money was an image so bleak it tightened my solar plexus into a burning gnarl.

But for my aunts, poker was an acceptable means of overcoming their distance. My mother and Van, for example, who lived in houses not more than ten feet apart, rarely spoke, and then mostly by accident when they would discover each other out in their adjoining backyards and awkwardness forced them to say something. A few words, perhaps a *Yak Tam*, or a chat about the lawn or the weather, or a bit of gossip about the increase in the price of vegetables they bought from the old man who came through the neighborhood sitting atop a horse-drawn green peddler's wagon with wide-spoked wooden wheels and loaded with produce he'd purchased to resell.

A short, stumpy man, whose face, lined with dirt-embedded creases, mapped his many hardscrabble years. He dressed every day in raggedy overalls, a faded black shirt buttoned too-tight at the collar which bunched up the skin beneath his chin, a frayed and fatigued black leather flat cap, the short brim worn bare and shiny from the many times he tipped it to his customers, a black leather vest he used to hold his tobacco and rolling papers, a pouch strapped to his waist as his bank, and ankle high black workman's boots he kept polished only over his arch and toes leaving the back crusted over with years. He confessed that he had bad feet and needed the best boots for their support.

No one knew if he was Jewish, but they all called him the Sheeny Man, an ethnic slur referring to immigrant Jews. But he brought vegetables to our door, so to that extent he was accepted. I'd wait excitedly to pet his horse, a weathered nag with a leather feed basket fixed over his snout and whose head always hung low so that he seemed sad. After purchases had been made and the man and his foodstuffs were out of sight, the women who remained out on the sidewalk, my mother and Van included, reviled him with, "Such a Jew. *Gruntowny Zyd*" (Thorough Jew)."

For all of their frivolity and laughter my relatives were more like an agglomeration of parts held together by blood and circumstance who would periodically come together and occupy the same space. Their practiced and honed rituals of conversation and weekly card playing gave the impression of connection. But none of them were true friends. They were family. If it hadn't been for their blood-bond, if they'd somehow met as strangers, the likelihood of their becoming close would have been low. Spontaneous intimacy was not part of their daily life. They relied on what they'd rehearsed because they knew nothing else. The result, conduct that was the fertile ground of loneliness: a loneliness buried deep in the past when they were still young and alive enough to feel it but had since been muzzled leaving only a terrifying whisper in their most private moments which they strove to silence.

Poker had created the foreground for a sense of belonging, devoid, however, of the bond that gives belonging its pleasure, security, and peace.

At nine years old, I could feel that barrenness, the draining effect of mechanical living; feel but not make sense of; feel in my body like a worm screwing itself into my every day. I know now but didn't then that when I was at a family gathering, like the card party, and I would begin to yawn, my need for large volumes of air was the first sign that I was falling inward, dropping into a blackness I thought was sleep. I accepted it as normal, or at least not suspicious, and I would, especially during Sunday mass, for example, succumb to the blackness to the point of not hearing anything, and only becoming aware of what had happened when my mother would poke me, frowning, and I would bolt back into an awareness of my surroundings.

I was only vaguely aware that these blackouts signaled my desire and need to connect, to belong, to recognize myself and be recognized as part of something, and they arose only when I felt most alone, most alienated. What little identity I possessed was adrift and floating. And no surprise, my night dreams were filled with vast, unpopulated, black and terrifying lonely spaces.

My loneliness was exacerbated by our neighborhood. There were thirteen boys living on our street, ranging in age from nine to twelve, constituting our own gang. We didn't have a name for it. When we talked among ourselves we simply referred to it as "our gang." We were not yet old enough to cause trouble, or at least not serious trouble. But our teachers, the Sisters of Saint Francis, themselves minimally educated, dry, haggard Old Country women whose devotion to Catholicism entailed a strict and brutal self-mortification, which included whipping themselves across the bare back with the white knotted cord that, as part of their habit, hung from their waist, condemned us for belonging to what they labeled as "Our Gang," which they thought was its formal name, and warned us that we were destined for an eternity in hell.

We did engage in mischief: petty theft, which always terrified me because I didn't want to disappoint my father; and vandalism, which made me sad because I personally knew the people who owned the properties we were trashing. But having been born on our street I was a member of the gang by default. I belonged, and belonging, even by default, gave me a slight yet comforting sense of identity.

But in truth I had no business thinking of myself as a gang member and I knew it. I wasn't tough or aggressive. But I didn't dare show weakness. So I was as rehearsed and mechanical as everyone else. Eventually, though, my lack of bravado exposed my differentness and led to my being kicked out of the gang, ostracized, an exile on my own block.

I watched the women play. Their chit chat commingled with their calling out what games would be played: deuces wild, straight five card stud, high-lo, and various others.

My mother talked about the church bingos and the pleasure she received from working them. She'd become very close with the pastor and he'd come to depend on her. My mother's devotion led to her running the bingos. But because of the misogyny prevalent in the community she could not be publicly acknowledged for fear of being seen as rising above the men, and the harassment she'd be put through for something she dearly loved doing wouldn't have been worth it. She didn't mind the lack of recognition because her closeness to the pastor allowed her access to church gossip no one else could know giving her a special sense of value and position.

With five kings—two kings and three wild cards: two red sevens and one one-eyed jack—my mother won the first pot. Irene's face flushed with exasperation, her nose and earlobes glowing like geraniums. She'd drawn a natural straight which was a winning hand in any normal game designed for knowledge, skill, and shrewdness, not some phony game for these *delikatne panie* (delicate ladies) a term of derision and disgust usually hurled at upper class socialites.

"Five kings," Irene snorted. "How the hell can you win a simple-minded game like this?"

"Simple-minded? Why did you keep raising?" Van countered. "You know the risk." Van's satisfaction, which she did not hide from Irene, began at her mouth and spread to her eyes and then covered her face.

"Feh," Irene glared as she gathered the cards to her. It was her deal and she announced with an authority that would crush any objection. "Five card draw, nothing wild." She organized the deck and began shuffling.

"Helcha, how are those two women next door doing, what's their name?" Blanche asked. She always had trouble remembering their names: not because she was incapable but because the way their father forced them to live frightened her.

Agnes and Zita, two spinsters, were known to everyone on the street as the *"stare siostry pokojówka,"* the old maid sisters. Agnes, whose small wiry frame, beaked nose, yellowish gray hair, and a shrill high-pitched voice that inspired the neighborhood nickname "Sea Gull," seemed to cry out when she spoke as though her vocal chords were being squeezed tight. When I saw her in the backyard, which was not often, she was nice enough, actually kind of sweet, but withdrawn as though she was always four seconds behind.

Zita, nicknamed Pie Face, resembled a pock-marked flat bread: deflated around the edges and puffed in the center, colorless except for a couple of splotches. Her body filled out an oval much like the antique picture frames that hung in our dining room exhibiting the portraits of my grandparents. I often saw her in her backyard waddling along the cement walkway from the house to the fence that marked the border between their yard and the alley where she'd stop, look down as though to locate her feet, turn and waddle back. I once asked her what she was doing. Her face went blank. Finally, a sterile smile appeared that showed her yellowing teeth, and she told me, "I'm praying. Don't you pray?"

Their father, Aleksandr—a square block of a man with broad shoulders, extra-large hands, thick neck, and a jaw that obstinately jutted out—gave the impression he was always poised for attack. Even his name incited hostility because he insisted on the Russian spelling, "Aleksandr," knowing that would be an affront to the other Poles in the neighborhood and an insult to their heritage. He indulged his judgment that they were *mniej niż* (less than) and not worthy of his time or concern.

His aggressive posture was accentuated by his hyper-orthodox Catholicism. He was a believer for several reasons. The first was devotional: he was, by character, a true believer which allowed for and supported his embrace of the black-and-white stance of "no other options but righteous obedience." And second, his personal reasons: to confirm the upright and virtuous status he claimed for himself among the men on our street, men who mocked him and called him *szalony święty*, crazy saint. He repeatedly told the story of Saint Alexander who was condemned to death for his faith and thrown into an arena of wild beasts, but the lions refused to attack and martyr him. Aleksandr felt he was in such a den of persecution living among lesser types, and that God would keep them at bay as a testament to Aleksandr's dedication to Holy Mother Church.

Even though he'd sired his two girls he was never comfortable with them because he said, "they make me jumpy." And he'd never given himself fully to his wife, who was long dead, or his marriage because he was partnered with God and His saints, which, as he insisted, was his only life.

He'd deliberately chosen the girls' names because, as he proudly announced, they were the names of saints and the first letters, A and Z, stood for the beginning and the end, birth and death. What he didn't know was that Saint Agnes is the patron saint of chastity, rape victims, and virgins, and Saint Zita is the patron saint of maids and domestic servants. Their names predestined them to the void in which they were raised and interred.

"They're no different, Blanche. You know." My mother checked her hand. "What a life. They never go anywhere, never do anything. And Agnes I...I don't know what she does because I never see her except sometimes when she hangs clothes on the line. Zita, she prays and prays and prays and nothing happens, nothing changes. Such a shame." My mother's description included her feelings about prayer, faith, and the Church, but she didn't have enough self-awareness or courage to realize the breadth of what she was saying.

"It's like being in jail," Blanche scowled, her lips curling with anger and contempt. "It's a sin, what that man does to them."

"Sin!?" Irene almost shouted, picking up her cards and fanning them out to read her hand. "It's criminal. He's a god damned criminal...I'll take two cards...the son-of-a-bitch."

With growing disinterest, I watched the women play for several hands. The longer I watched the farther away they seemed as though they were fading. I laid my head on the back of the chair, closed my eyes, and in that darkness, a darkness I had come to love for its simplicity and privacy, I wondered how far they would have to drift away before they disappeared entirely. Would they disappear? Or would I go blind?

Utterly unexpected, that last question ricocheted off the invisible walls of my internal escape reflecting back at me like wild-eyed faces, mouths gaping, angry for what I dared wonder. The thought of blindness scared me back to the table as a sudden roar of laughter exploded upward from the basement.

Even though it was not unusual for the men to shout and cheer when one of them played well, and cuss and attack each other when someone made a bonehead play, their burst of laughter startled me, and the women as well.

"Somebody did something right," Van stood slamming her cards against the table mimicking what we'd all seen the men do. "They think they're so important."

"*Głupie jak dzieci*" (Silly like children), Blanche joined in. "You tell them and tell them and what…what?"

"*To tylko zabawa*," my mother spoke up, defending The Brothers. "They're just having fun."

Her identification with The Brothers anchored her place-in-the-world which otherwise was thin at best. In most instances, when any one of the women mocked the men, my mother took it personally, as though she was being mocked, shaming her Brothers-based loyalty. But this time, surrounded by the family women and their mockery, her defense was more apology than vindication.

The way the women treated the men added to my mother's ambivalence about getting together. But our house was the seat of Anna's authority and emotional security and she insisted, overtly by command and subtly by emotional extortion, that her family stay together, a responsibility and task she succinctly assigned to my mother. With Anna living upstairs, our house was to remain the hub, which translated into various grades of visiting, from dropping over without warning to Friday evening card parties and whatever else in between.

As a young girl, Anna's sense of personal value and esteem had been based on her fervent desire to entrust her life to God. But her fierce dedication was not without its own venality. In her most private self she had had concerns about pride and spiritual greed: pride because her devotion to the Mass was unmatched by any other girl or adult in her village, a personal quality that influenced her to hold her head just that much higher whenever she was in public; spiritual greed because she saw her unfailing attendance as a sign of God's desire to be near her rather than vice versa, and she believed her every genuflection as well as her daily communion roused His desire that much more. Her relationship with God was, in large part, an accounting, a spiritual tallying of her value and attractiveness to Him. But she suffered the worry that her motive was not the most pure, because love of God and nothing else was supposed to animate her reverence. However, she reasoned, even though pride and greed were two of the Seven Deadly Sins, God, out of the unfathomable depth of His benevolence and love, would forgive her and bring her into His Heart.

But her life in Detroit was hardly proof of being cherished by God. More like He rejected her. If she had only been allowed to become a nun, to serve Holy Mother Mary and to be there every day for God the Father's need and spiritual pleasure rather than Antoni, whose simple-minded lust became more and more repulsive, she could have looked forward to a beautiful life and her reward in Heaven. As she brooded over what had not happened, and what might have happened, she felt deprived of a life that was her destiny: a life she was fit for and deserved. She had proven herself and the world had robbed her of it. Robbed, plundered, raped were the words she could not keep out of her mind. And none of her prayers consoled her with an answer to her constant question: "*Dlaczego Boże?*" Why, God?

Eventually, and imperceptibly, she reached a different conclusion. Instead of serving, since serving had long passed, she was owed attention and recognition for the life that never happened, and she expected the debt to be paid in the form of fawning, flattering, gushing, and most important, humble ingratiation by The Brothers, delivered mostly by the youngest two, Ari and Chez. When The Brothers did not pay their due, the darkness that settled in Anna's eyes was enough to remind them of their lapse of respect and bring them back into line.

Nothing my mother ever did could be enough for Anna so my mother might as well have been invisible. She never received so much as a nod of appreciation or acknowledgement because, in Anna's gratuitous and princessly indulgent mind, the work my mother did around the house, cleaning, cooking, keeping the family together, was raised beyond the secular status of mere duty to the spiritual level of moral obligation: to be performed without complaint as respect owed to God and mother.

Suddenly and even more stridently another burst of laughter from the men in the basement pierced the women's table causing my mother to leap to her feet and turn toward the kitchen and back stairs.

"Where are you going?" Irene asked.

"Downstairs to see if they need anything." She watched the words fly out of her mouth, and although they were hers, she felt as though they belonged to someone else. Of course the men didn't need anything and did not need her, but she'd already said it and froze, with her back to the others waiting for what they would say.

"You act like their servant, Helen," Van began the reproof.

"They don't need another mother," Irene added.

Van and Irene were right. My mother knew it. She'd been caught—again.

Van couldn't help herself from driving home the point my mother had heard many times before. "They're drinking like alcoholics and what are you gonna do? Go down there and give them more?"

"*Proszę*," my mother half-turned back and whispered, "Please," as though she was afraid someone might hear and discover her; discover how she kowtowed to the men.

"*Proszę*, my ass," Irene snapped.

Mary Therese fiddled inside her purse.

"*Cicho, cicho być*" (Be quiet) Blanche barked unexpectedly stopping the whole scene. She was hardly a barker. "Don't punish her," she said solidly and with a surprising authority.

"What?" Van flared. "Are *you* gonna serve them?" Her eyes narrowed into slits fixed on Blanche.

"Be quiet, Van." Blanche held her ground for a moment and then looked away.

Satisfied with her triumph, "*Fffttt,*" Van hissed her dismissal and sat down.

"Hey," Vi grabbed the attention, "what'a ya got?"

Van and Blanche had folded. Mary Therese watched but did not play. Irene had a pair of Aces.

"Helen?" Vi asked.

"*Nie mam nic,*" (I have nothing), my mother said quietly, standing next to the table. She actually had a good hand, two pair—Queens and Eights—but she didn't want to bring more attention to herself. "*Nic,*" she waved Vi off.

"Then I win," Vi beamed. "Two pair, Fours and Threes."

"God damn it. Are we gonna play cards here and focus, or what?" Irene threw her cards into the center of the table.

"And it's my deal," Vi laughed, her bouncing breasts accentuating her pleasure.

Aunt Vi, the most attractive of all the women and whose smile was always radiant if sometimes a bit too impeccable, caught and held my attention. Her pleasure at winning was sincere: not because she'd defeated the others but because she genuinely delighted in such minor triumphs—when a pie crust she was baking turned out light and flaky; when the color of a new sweater exactly matched her nail polish; when her husband Chez washed and polished their Buick and she could clearly see her smile in the luster.

But it was Vi's breasts that seemed to be giggling, hop and flop, that brought Janice's little nubs flashing in my imagination. Janice wasn't at the table. I hadn't noticed until that moment that she'd remained in the front room. I turned to see that she was engrossed in an album of photographs we kept in the bottom drawer of one of the end tables: memories of the family and neighborhood my mother would look through when she was sad or felt lost. I wondered how Janice had found it, because I had believed it was a private secret volume and I took offense at her intrusion. How dare Janice sit there, out in the open, casually snooping through what was so personal?

My baby pictures were scattered throughout the pages. She would see me naked in a variety of poses throughout my first two years. I never saw her naked. Never saw her chest the way she could see mine. And why wasn't she at the table? Who did she think she was, something special? That was the first time, the very first time I felt angry at Janice's standoffishness. 'Who does she think she is?' I thought. 'I greeted her when she came in. And what did she do? She was mean. She didn't even look at me. And now she's looking at pictures of me.'

I'd so wanted to touch Janice's breasts and now I wanted to slap her. I wanted to rip the album out of her hands and tell her off. Then I'd hide the album so no one would know where to find it. It was mine not hers. Ours not hers. Mine.

The next time my mother looked for it she wouldn't be able to find it. She'd ask me, "Have you seen the picture album?" I would tell her the whole story: how Janice had violated us; how I put her in her place; how I protected our privacy; and I'd retrieve the album so that my mother and I could sit next to each other on the couch and spend the afternoon, close and intimate. We'd have something special. Very special. And my mother would be grateful.

"Jim," I heard my name called from somewhere very far away. The call was not strong enough to take my focus away from Janice the prowler, Janice the cold intruder, Janice the mean and uncaring trespasser.

"Jim," this time closer. Insistent. But there still was Janice who was now looking at me, staring at me. Of course, she would be staring, my name was being called. But my name, the sound of it, seemed to be floating in some space not wholly mine.

My face flushed with embarrassment at having been caught by Janice. She surely must have known what I was thinking. Suddenly I wanted to flee, to disappear, to confess.

"Jim!" like a thunder clap that burst right over my head violently jerking me out of myself, I heard my mother demand, "What are you doing?"

I was certain I had been caught, exposed, made public just like my naked infant body for everyone to see, to gape at.

"Huh?" slipped out.

"What are you doing?" My mother, still standing in the doorway between the dining room and the kitchen, was even more insistent. Instead of Janice, I became the wrongdoer. The finger of shame no longer pointed to Janice but to me. "What are you doing?" she charged, more of a conviction of my crime than a question, and she welcomed the release from the intensity the women had directed at her.

"Huh? I...What? Nothing. What? Nothing."

I looked back to Janice and she was again into the album.

"High-lo," Vi announced as the next game of cards. It was another women's game in which the person with the highest hand won seventy-percent of the pot and the one with the lowest hand took the remainder.

I heard myself exhale, grateful to Vi for drawing my mother's attention away from me, and only then realized I'd been holding my breath.

I looked back to Janice. To my surprise, I could see the album didn't belong to us. It turned out to be a memory book, very much like my mother's, which Irene had brought to entertain Janice who did not like cards, neither playing nor watching.

A third uproar from the basement filled the room. The women looked to my mother who stood for a moment in silence, back in the spotlight, her insides taut, wanting to go to the men and her increasing embarrassment for wanting to do so.

"Well?" Irene asked my mother without hostility. She just wanted an answer so the hand Vi was already dealing could go forward.

"Ya, ya," my mother half-smiled in forced capitulation. Feeling tightness in her neck and shoulders she returned to her seat at the table. She tried to ease her tension with the thought that, after all, she was female and her place was with the women. But she knew her justification was hollow at best.

Vi, who had already looked at her hand, cooed, "I love High-Lo." She could never hold her cards close to her chest, both literally and figuratively, so the others pretty much knew when she had a good hand. "Van, how many cards do you want?"

Another burst from the basement, not as raucous but still loud. I was shaken by it. Should I stay or leave? Should I watch poker or go to the men?

My body moved, as though by its own will and design, and all of a sudden I was standing. I felt like an observer inside an event, a Jim inside of Jim watching Jim. My body walked into the kitchen, stared at the door to the back porch, decided against it, made a left turn, entered the bathroom, and locked the door. Then I locked the second door which led to the staircase that accessed the upstairs apartment where *busia* Anna lived.

The bathroom was the only room in the house that could be locked. But it was also the main passageway between the first and second floors and always susceptible to someone knocking. For Anna to come down in the night required something serious, perhaps catastrophic, because once she'd decided to go to bed she'd hobble up the stairs leaving behind the standing order that she was not to be disturbed.

She never cared for books, except for her prayer manual, which she claimed to read every night. Ironically, she stopped reading the Bible years before, arguing that prayers were the best way to heaven. My mother believed Anna had rejected the Bible because an excerpt from it had been used by the village priest to berate her when she refused to give up hope of the beautiful young man she'd fallen in love with.

Anna had already clumped her way up and I could almost certainly count on not hearing any knocks from the second door. But one of the women at the poker table might need to use the toilet, or even one of the men if the basement stall was occupied. The door to the kitchen was definitely a threat, but the swirl of feelings making me dizzy left me addled, enough to override the risk.

I sat on the floor, back against the tub, and closed my eyes. The dizziness advanced to a nausea I'd felt only once before.

Two years earlier, when I was just seven, my father was away at work and my mother and Anna headed out for the corner grocery leaving me alone. I'd decided to find out why my uncles always said, "Damn that's good," or "Shiiit that's good," when they drank Seven Crown. So I gently lifted the bottle out from its storage place under the kitchen sink as though it might explode, shards piercing my body leaving me on the floor soaked in condemning bourbon.

The nuns warned us that God was always watching and He knew our every move. I could see Sister Mary Jadviga's dark face, her eyes closed into slits intensifying the horror I would experience should I fall into sin because "God knows you. You can't get away. God knows what you're thinking." Other nuns used the same threat but Jadwiga added a personal twist: "And if He stopped thinking about you even for just one second, you'd go out of existence."

I unscrewed the cap and waited, bottle in hand. It did not explode.

Nothing happened.

I raised the bottle with a hushed expectation that what I was about to do might conjure the Devil from his abysmal den and bring down the wrath of God. But my quaking fear aside, I knew I was going forward. I had to know what was so special in that bottle.

First I placed my nostrils right to the top of the bottle and sniffed. A biting sting shocked my nose and sent my head into a full SNAP recoil. I couldn't believe what I was smelling, terribly foul and genuinely painful. Looking back, I wonder why that hadn't been enough to stop me. Instead I blinked hard, hoping to stop the sting and clear away the tears and the blur it had caused.

A charge of defiance pushed me forward. I would not be distracted nor deflected. I'd entered a world without preparation, both the shock which none of my uncles seemed to experience, and the defiance that curled up through my torso from some place unknown.

My defiance surged again. I raised the bottle to my mouth, trying to ignore the stench of the Seven Crown. I filled my mouth about a quarter full, felt the prickly bourbon stings, and swallowed. It was even fouler than I'd imagined. There had to be more to it than a bitter taste and a stinging mouth. I drank again. But the fire in my mouth ignited again followed by burning confusion. Had my Uncle Ari lied? My father? The rest of them? How could they like this stuff?

Or was it me? Was there something wrong with me?

I swallowed my third round as a test. Perhaps I would like it and then know what they all meant. I didn't. Not at all. I felt heat in my ears and face. And more tears. This time they rose not from the bourbon but from my deep disappointment. Was it me? Something wrong with me? Why didn't I like it? Wasn't I a man? An ancient shapeless ache flooded my body, a feeling of loss and desolation, of loneliness and displacement.

Slowly a velvety darkness slithered up my back, over the top of my head, and settled in behind my eyes. I felt like I was sinking and utterly alone. Then I heard my mother and Anna coming along the side of the house and I lunged back to alertness. I quickly capped the bottle, returned it under the sink, ran to my room, and shut the door. On my back, spread out across the bed, the ceiling began to spin and I panicked. Then came the nausea.

Now, in the locked bathroom leaning against the tub, my nausea became stronger and I shuddered at the thought that the spinning would be next. I opened my eyes with the hope that I could escape it. I didn't.

I remembered the empty aloneness I'd felt two years before and could feel myself sliding back into that gloom.

My eyelids became heavy, dragging me in and down. I used my fingers to keep my lids from closing. It worked. As long as I forced my eyelids open the spinning slowed, the nausea receded, until finally I became still.

I felt the stillness flow through me, coating my insides like a second skin: gentle, without demand or direction; smooth as though it had been buffed free of imperfections.

After a moment, I heard a thumping: a full-toned, resonant, deep thump, like footsteps sounding on a wood plank floor covered with carpet. Was Anna coming down? I listened closely. No. Not Anna. Was it one of the men coming up? Not that either. The kitchen floor would squeak when someone walked over it, a squeak I'd become familiar with and I heard nothing.

The slow rhythmic methodical almost melodic thumping continued.

I sat as still as I could trying to determine where the thump was coming from, now deeper and more resonant.

Instead of a flat sound that began and ended, the thumps seemed to radiate, like ripples in a pool, each thump a stone in water and the ripples its undulating voice.

I closed my eyes to remove any distraction and my head fell to my chest. *Thump. Thump. Thump.*

Then I heard it: my heart. The thumping was my own heart: the deep base resonant thump of my own heart. I'd never noticed my own heartbeat before and almost jumped up from the fright of it. Bizarre. Macabre. I was inside my own guts.

At first I thought it was a sin to hear my own heartbeat. Too personal. Too intimate. Too much body. We were taught our body is our temple, but not a temple I should walk into: a sacred place to be revered not trespassed sitting on a bathroom floor. In my concern, I shifted and discovered that moving made the thumping disappear. But as soon as I'd become still, there it was again. My own heart.

I'd often used the bathroom as a hideaway. Stepping into the tub I'd pull the shower curtain closed to create a refuge. I'd open the spigot, adjust the water temperature, and sit on the tub floor under the spigot, my legs brought up close to my chest. With my hands, I'd direct the hot stream to various parts of my body. I loved that solitude. I wouldn't have called it that then but my closed-off secret bathtub chamber was more a place of my own than my bedroom.

I considered pulling the shower curtain and getting in, but, because there were so many people in the house I didn't dare risk getting under the spigot only to have someone knock, demanding to be let in. So I stayed on the floor leaning against the tub listening to my heart.

As I listened a vivid image rose behind my closed eyes: my heart, suspended, thumping; chambers opening and closing; blood gushing; life pulsing; but no arteries. Blood gushing, but no blood ways to the rest of my body. As for the rest of my insides, I saw nothing. Empty. Vacant. My body contained a floating heart. Nothing else. Nothing. No veins. No bones. Nothing.

My head fell back, resting on the top of the tub wall and, rather than being shocked or frightened by what my imagination had conjured, I felt calm and quiet, as though I were home. I sighed with the relief and protection of a place I knew, a place that knew me, a place away from the world, away from others. I felt a thrill at the thought of being distant from others, of actually preferring that distance, the comfort and seclusion of that distance.

I drew in a deep breath, held it for a few seconds, and released it with a sigh. For a moment, I felt what I would now call love, but then I had no words for it: a pleasing warmth I was certain was pleased with me, a love of me for me, streaming throughout all of me—my face, my toes, the back of my head, and I, like my heart, was floating.

An odd thought drifted into my awareness: "Am I floating in the bathroom," I whispered.

Opening my eyes to re-connect with the room I was not sure what to expect. Nothing had changed: the toilet to my right, the wash basin to my left, and the door to the kitchen directly across. Just as they had always been.

I closed my eyes and the image of my suspended heart began to cloud over: not in large puffy swaths but like the droplets in a fog, emerging out of nowhere, twitching, restless, on the move. My heart slowly, peacefully disappeared behind a soft radiance of color, the drops sunlit from behind like the images I'd seen of the Sacred Heart of Jesus.

The thumping, which had grown weaker, stopped, and the color field began to drift away, contracting into a smaller and smaller space as it receded, as though being swallowed by the surrounding dark, and I slipped into a deeper, even quieter reverie.

The darkness enveloped me like a blanket, like a caring friend, and I felt myself moving through it. I could feel it whisper past my ears like a gentle, wordless, coaxing voice, carrying me along.

In the distance, something appeared. Alluring. Magnetic. Pulling me. A light. A pin spot of blue-gray light. I would find out what it was, not by choice but necessity, because I was speeding toward it.

As I moved closer to the light the surrounding darkness began to break up, splitting into long thin slivers with the light slipping through. The stronger the light appeared the faster I was moving until suddenly the remaining darkness vanished and I was thrust, almost launched into a vast drab field of fruit trees without color. Desperate. Dismal. Desolate. Yet vivid, lifelike.

Diseased trees were scattered across the scene: gray leaves corrupt with holes and ragged edges; parched and shriveled veins cracked and open; their once lush and vibrant surfaces now dingy and barren, covered with worms; trees still standing but bent over with fruit that had long since rotted; fruit that should have dropped centuries ago, eons ago, gashed with age and decay, bulging with swollen pustules, oozing thick unnatural juices.

Faces drifted above and through the horror-field like ragged, threadbare scarves whisked aloft by an unnatural wind: some laughing, some shrieking, some stark without expression.

The blue-gray light, itself patchy, wavered as though it too was trying to escape this place. The stench caught in my nose: a bitter, rancid smell that hung in thick, clotted air. I couldn't breathe. Try as I might I could not make my body work to take in a breath of air. I wanted to scream but couldn't. I wanted to flee but couldn't. I wanted to die but couldn't.

And just then I felt a sharp pointed pain explode at the back of my head and I was flung back into the bathroom gasping for breath. Even eyes-open my breathing was strained, as though I had to draw in the air from some great distance, and it required more physical strength than I had the capacity for.

Finally, without warning, as if someone had opened a dam holding back masses of air, breath flooded my lungs with force and I felt punched. I gasped again, grabbing the back of my head to ease the pain. While in that nightmare field, that putrid, loathsome hell where death should have reigned but didn't, I had unconsciously raised my head away from the top of the tub, apparently to get away from that scene of damnation, and then dropped it smashing the base of my head into the unforgiving porcelain.

The pain that pulsed was real, very real, in the very real bathroom of my house in Detroit. I felt its burn reach from the back of my head into my eyes looking for a route to escape. My eye-pain was a blessing, a very real blessing. At least I was out of that deathless horror.

I stood, my head throbbing, and looked into the mirror on the medicine cabinet above the wash basin. I was relieved to see that it was my real face there in the mirror. I felt my face just to be sure and the figure in the mirror respectfully followed my movement. It was real. But what I saw in the mirror scared me more than anything: the image of a terrified, bewildered boy.

I opened the cold-water spigot and splashed my face getting a bit more hold of myself. Then I walked to the toilet, lowered the top lid, and sat.

What had happened?

"Jimush," my mother knocked, springing me to my feet so fast that the dizziness momentarily returned. My mother! Did she know? Did she? And yet I welcomed her voice, an anchor from the world out there, a world which, at the moment, was far more inviting than the deathscape I had fallen into.

"What?"

"Are you okay?"

"What?"

"I heard some noises. Are you okay?"

"I'm okay."

My mother's interest in me had always floated from intense to meager to absent depending upon her own need. Sometimes I was her sole focus. At other times I was invisible.

"I heard some noise," she insisted.

"Not in here."

"Are you finished?"

"Almost."

"Okay."

The kitchen floor squeaked as she walked back to the poker game.

My breathing eased. The pain in my head began to subside. I remembered Janice and the memory book and leaving the dining room table in a sort of trance, ending up in the bathroom. As my memory cleared I began to better locate myself both in the room and within my own body. I remembered my heart and listened for the thumping. Just being conscious in the room, seeing the tub, feeling the plastic shower curtain, recognizing the narrow radiator on the opposite wall, and the wash basin with drops splashed on its edges drove my heart back into my body where it thumped silently.

"What was I doing?" I muttered. "Oh, I remember…going downstairs."

I stood for another minute, still in the grip of fearsome wonderment, and decided to follow through to the basement. I unlocked and opened the door to see Janice waiting to use the room.

"Are you okay?" She was staring again.

"Why?"

"I don't know. Are you done?"

"Yeah." I walked past her to the back door and stepped onto the back porch.

Beer Barrel and Brutality

As I looked through the porch window, the back yard, brushed by the last streams of daylight, danced like a mirage, its shapes and colors quivering. For a moment, I thought I could see through it to something behind, as though the hazy scene had been painted on the outer side of the window and beyond it the real back yard waited for me to discover.

I pressed my nose against the glass. Was it there? Whatever it was I hoped for? No. The back yard just lay there closing down for the night: a green lawn blackened by the oncoming darkness; flower beds whose colors were vanishing in the night shade; a chain-link fence installed to set a boundary, to establish an identity, and to protect us against the fear triggered by a number of home robberies at the other end of the block near the steel pickling plant; and three wire clothes lines strung between two metal posts each in the shape of a cross reminding me of the crucifix.

I'd wanted something different but it wasn't there. Just the backyard as I'd always known it.

Propelled by a sigh, I pulled away from the glass. For a moment, literally a micro-second, my feet seemed to be far away, so far away that I might be a mile tall. And then, in a twitch, everything reverted to normal. The distortion was not unfamiliar but this time it was safe. I didn't feel the risk of being sucked in.

Catching my side-glance vision, light from the utility pole across the alley and two houses away ricocheted off an ice cube in the *beczka*, the half-barrel which had been placed on the landing, five steps down, where the aluminum and glass door, what we called the "outside" door, opened to the backyard. The *beczka* was filled with beer for the night's supply.

A sorrowful ache rose in my chest and hung there.

An hour before everyone arrived my father had given me the job of filling the *beczka* with bottles of Strohs. He'd gone out to an ice company, a remnant in our neighborhood of the icebox days when blocks of ice were needed to keep food refrigerated. He brought back three large bags of ice cubes and dumped them into the *beczka* and set a partial case of Strohs next to it.

He called me to the back porch and ordered, "I want you to get at least twelve bottles into that ice. And make sure you bury them deep." I wondered why he hadn't put the bottles in before he dumped the ice which would have made the job a lot easier. Was he testing me or had he made a mistake? I couldn't decide but said, "Okay. I will," and tried to let it go at that.

He nodded, his gaze turning inward, and descended the steps into the basement.

But I couldn't let go of the thought that my father, MY FATHER, had made a mistake. Rather than humanizing him in my eyes—seeing him as a man rather than the demigod I'd crafted him to be, rather than recognizing not just that he was capable of mistakes but acknowledging his vulnerability, how fiercely he struggled not to make them—he scared me. My father didn't do that sort of thing. He just didn't. But then he did. He put the ice in before the bottles.

For a moment I felt lost, abandoned. Ice before bottles! I couldn't believe it, or, rather, didn't know how to believe it. I'd never imagined such a thing: not even the possibility.

But there it was. I felt my face redden with anger, a puzzling, unintelligible anger. How could he have done that?

I know now what I didn't know then: my recognition of what he had done, ice before the bottles, penetrated his façade, or rather the face he and I had fabricated together. I didn't know then there was even such a thing as a façade, which made my anger even more confusing and frightening. All that I knew was the discomfort I felt. He had let me down.

Although he was a perfectionist, a relentless perfectionist whose authority, presence, and power rested upon his insistence for perfection, he was not perfect. Although he lived by the principle "measure twice cut once," and it had always paid off when he undertook jobs around the house, at least I'd thought so, it became clear, and undeniable, that he did make mistakes, although very few, a personality characteristic The Brothers admired and resented him for, especially Julli.

Whenever Julli worked on the exterior of his house next door nothing he did could be hidden, and there was always something to do around the houses in our eighty-year-old neighborhood—paint, plumbing, electric, woodwork.

One summer Julli decided he would replace the tongue-and-groove flooring on his front porch. Over the years, the winter snow and sleet had combined with the summer's heat to cause the gray paint on the wood slats to blister and peel exposing them to decay and deterioration. My father had advised Julli to first apply a coat of primer/sealer before painting to protect the wood from the elements. But, true to Julli's disposition, he had refused directions and the rot on the wood edges had become obvious.

Julli decided that, rather than sand down the floor slats and rotting edges and cover them with sealer and paint, the flooring of the entire porch had to go. He fancied himself a craftsman but in truth he was impulsive and a blunderer, the more care the repair demanded the more Julli relied on Strohs as his workmate.

Things weren't going well with the porch. Driven by his impulsivity, Julli had attacked the porch with more frenzy than focus. During his first afternoon, thoroughly enjoying the banging and the ripping, he'd torn out every floor slat before he realized he'd made it a lot more difficult to reconstruct the porch floor because all that remained were the steps, the joists of the porch skeleton, and a gaping hole. Embarrassed by the upheaval he'd created, Julli's mind locked up except for the shame that pounded him for being such a boy. "God damn it," he growled under his breath. He raised his Strohs and *"Bowhn!"* He downed a long, reliable chug.

Coming home from work, my father parked his black 1949 Fleetline Chevrolet sedan at the curb in front of our house. Its name "Fleetline" best described its design, a sleek unbroken curve sweeping from the windshield to the back bumper, a match for the top of his polished Oxford shoes glistening below the cuffs of his factory work pants. The contrast exposed my father's eccentricity, his attempt to belong somewhere else, to something else.

The word "Fleetline" gave the impression of status and meaning, suggesting aerodynamics and flight. But in fact, it was just another Chevy, part of General Motors' upper-lower to middle-middle class offerings.

Even though he couldn't help but see Julli's mess, he said nothing, and walked between the houses, his contempt brewing as he came in through the outside door. The right side of his upper lip pushed up and to the right as though it was headed for his ear: the sure sign of his contempt.

"Your brother," he snarled at my mother, "is an idiot. You can't tell him anything."

"Ed, Ed, leave him alone. Let him be."

"The way he's working on that porch is all wrong. He doesn't listen."

"You know he won't Ed," my mother said softly hoping to defuse him. "That's just Julli."

"That's just being a fool. I can't stand to see…" He held in whatever was pushing at him.

"See what?" my mother asked. As soon as she did she knew she'd regret asking.

"He's like the rest of your brothers only he's the worst."

"So it's my brothers now."

"Don't start, Helen. You know I'm right about this."

He was right. She knew it.

Whenever my father took on a repair job around our house he did it with patience and deliberation, planning ahead, considering and reconsidering his options until he decided on the best approach. My mother was grateful because, most of the time, there would be little if any mess in the house and no distress between them. She could count on his concentration and skill to finish the job perfectly as long as she left him alone.

None of The Brothers cared about work like my father did. They preferred the camaraderie of joining together, drinking, horsing around, and getting done whatever job they'd been called to help with—to whatever degree. Their work was never negligent, but it certainly was never perfect. And that galled my father.

"What do you want to do, Eddie? You want to talk to him? Go talk to him. You know I don't like to hear you pick on him. So go talk."

"Yeah. And if I do I know what you'll be thinking. I can see it on your face."

He was right again. She was angry and compelled to defend The Brothers no matter what they did, most especially against my father's contempt.

"Jesus, Eddie. Leave me alone. Go do what you have to do."

She disappeared through the outside door, grabbing a broom on the way, and cast herself into sweeping the sidewalk along the fence dividing our yard from Julli's next door. Sweeping was something she knew she could control and succeed at.

As she swept, my father stepped out onto the enclosed back porch and watched her through the window. He could see her lips moving. She was talking to herself and he wondered what she might be saying. A flash of hurt forced his eyelids down into a blink and then open only half way. He knew where her allegiance lay. It was not with him. Another blink and he walked through the house, out the front door, and watched, from his own front porch, what Julli was up to.

Standing between two chest-high floor joists Julli wrestled a six-foot length of board at the end of the porch nearest our house working its tongue into the groove of the only other one he'd nailed in place. He popped four three-and-a-half inch 16-penny nails into his mouth, pulled out a fifth nail from his carpenter's belt and was set to hammer, all the while feeling my father's eyes watching.

The height of the joist forced Julli to raise his arm at an angle that made hammering awkward at best. As he brought the hammer down it glanced off the nail head sending it rocketing toward our house, clinking as it hit the concrete walkway, coming to a stop right where my father was standing.

"How's it going, Julli?"

Julli knew full well how it was going and felt judged and belittled by the seeming innocence of my father's question.

"It's okay. It's going fine," never looking up.

"Need any help?"

"Listen Ketchup," Julli spit the other nails out of his mouth and shot back, "it's my fucking porch and I'll do it whatever fucking way I want. Okay?"

My father would rather have shredded Julli for his disregard, not just of my father but for the terrible job he was doing, his tantrum, and his unnecessary profanity, but he held his tongue. However, he could not prevent his right upper lip from rising.

Julli held his gaze, an alpha-beta stare down, then diverted his eyes, lifted himself out of the hole, picked up his Strohs from the top step, stomped down the remaining five to the sidewalk and disappeared along the far side of the house. "I could kill that son-of-a-bitch," he muttered as he strode to the backyard.

My father remained standing on the porch, an ache in his neck pulling his head back. As he dropped his head forward, pressing his chin down to his chest, he couldn't avoid noticing a deep sigh: not one smooth intake of breath but three small ones that rippled up from his gut.

He shut his eyes, and, suddenly, as though he was across the street looking back, he saw himself on the front porch not of his own house but his wife's mother's house and didn't know what he was doing there.

His mind went blank.

He worked as a tool-and-die designer and was considered an expert, the man to whom everyone brought the toughest problems which he never failed to solve. But when it came to his personal life he was out of his element. He couldn't tolerate the ambiguities: his inability to nail down and hold what he was feeling and get it to give up something he could act on. When it came to his work problems he said he always trusted his gut, but when it came to his family the affinity between gut and feelings never crossed his mind. And since his mind was blank he turned and went back inside.

On pinochle and poker nights, whether in summer or winter, the *beczka* sat on the back porch landing between two sets of steps: five steps down from the kitchen door to the landing, followed by four steps to the basement door. During the winter the back porch, which was not insulated, would become very cold. "Why put the *beczka* there?" the women argued.

"Because it's half-way between you women upstairs and the basement."

"That makes no sense," Van countered. "We almost never drink beer, and even if we did we could put some bottles in the refrigerator up in the kitchen."

She was clearly right but, rather than admit the fallacy of their thinking, the men gave her a what-do-you-know look and dismissed her in a self-righteous huff.

Preparing for the arrival of my relatives, I opened the case of Strohs my father had set on the landing, pulled it close to the *beczka*, and began by pushing a handful of cubes to one side intending to place the first bottle into the gap. But as I made the wedge in the ice and turned back to the case for a bottle I heard the surrounding cubes shift and fill the space. Never having watched any of the adults load the tub with bottles, I was surprised.

I tried again in another part of the tub, this time pushing more ice than before. Same result.

After trying a different strategy, twisting the bottles into the pile, bottoms first, I quickly realized that the density of the packed ice wouldn't allow it, so I had to be careful. All I needed to do was break one and I'd have the raspy odor of beer and ineptitude all over the back porch. I could just see my father's right upper lip.

I considered inserting the bottles cap first thinking the narrower circumference at the top would make it easier but then thought, 'Their bottoms will show.' I chuckled at the idea of their bottoms sticking up in the air. I was, after all, nine.

Baffled, I sat on the step nearest the tub and wondered what my father would say.

It wasn't often he trusted me with a job without first laying out the precise way I was to go forward, so I wondered again why the ice went in before the bottles. But this was an opportunity to please him, maybe even make him proud. I had to do a good job.

An alarm went off in my head. He could come out of the basement at any second and I didn't want to be caught sitting there, and worse, not knowing what to do. So I knelt between the tub and the beer case, pulling the case even closer. Then I made a gap in the ice, keeping my left hand in it while reaching into the case with my right for a bottle to shove into the tub.

When I reached toward the case with my right hand my left hand moved jostling the ice causing it to fall back into the gap. Not nearly as good an idea as I'd hoped.

Finally, I realized that I could lay a bottle on top of the ice pile, shift the cubes with both hands, and quickly move the bottle into the opening.

Great. It worked. Bottle number one.

A full case of Strohs held twenty-four bottles. Three had been previously removed. With one in the *beczka*, that left twenty. Now that I had a method I was determined to get them all in.

After the sixth bottle my hands were cold, but I persisted. Four more and the cold in my hands changed to pin pricks. I reached to the case for one more bottle and, because of the pain, I almost dropped it. I had to reach out to catch it. Gulping a breath, I made a yelping sound.

I froze, tilting my head toward the basement door, listening with all the concentration I could mobilize for any sound that would alert me that my father had heard my cry. I thought I heard him coming and snapped-to maneuvering the bottle in my hand toward the ice. But the door remained closed. So I placed the bottle on top of the pile and sat back, relieved.

Just then the door opened and my father caught me sitting. Frowning as he came toward me, he looked to the tub and counted the ten bottles I'd succeeded in placing, and the last one lying across the top of the pile. Then he noticed my red, stinging hands which I was clutching together.

"Your hands cold?" he asked.

"Uh huh."

"Eleven bottles?"

"Uh huh."

With hands twice the size of mine and much much stronger, he scooped a fistful of ice away from the side of the *beczka* and, holding the rest of the ice at bay, he shoved the eleventh bottle into the space and covered it almost completely.

"That's enough." He turned to me with a slight smile. "Good job."

Good job! My father's highest compliment. He shook his head slightly as though to say "Yes."

I became speechless. 'Good job?' I thought. 'Good job!'

My father looked at me, his smile evident. He waited for a response. He so rarely gave credit for anyone's work I didn't know what to say. Every word I'd ever known, every sound I'd ever made, fled. All I could do was stare.

His smile slowly shifted into a frown which frightened me. I couldn't help feeling I'd done something wrong, followed by a sense of guilt which I felt often, mostly with my mother and Anna.

As we sat there, face to face, I realized he wasn't angry. He was disappointed. Hurt. He had given me his best gift and I couldn't receive it. I wanted to but didn't know how.

'Good job?!' I thought.

I could still feel the sharp sting in my hands, especially my fingertips. My shoulders were tight. My stomach ached. I was empty. Hollow. Lacking.

Those two words repeated over and over, 'Good job. Good job. Good job.'

My father's disappointed hurt was replaced by a blank, almost featureless face, a mask. Empty, as though he mirrored back to me who I was. I wanted to speak, to say "wow," or "really" but I couldn't.

His face shifted again. He'd made a decision. He rose and slowly, heavily went back into the house.

'Good job.'

The pin pricks in my hands hurt worse than ever.

As I looked away from the *beczka* and stared out through the porch window feeling a weight in my chest, I heard Janice leave the bathroom, heard the floor squeak, and berated myself for not having shut the kitchen door. I heard her stop, half way through the kitchen and turned to see what she was doing.

"Are you okay?" she asked.

I felt ashamed remembering how wrong I'd been about the picture album but even so I didn't want to talk to her. I didn't trust that she really wanted to know what I was feeling, so I said, "Yeah," curt, pointed, dismissive. I wanted to be alone.

"*Tsk*," Janice shot back and headed toward the front room.

I turned back to the window. The darkening backyard was just the same as it had always been, no different. I was angry. I wanted something new to be there, something I hadn't seen before. I didn't know what. I didn't know why. The more I thought about it, the more I wanted it, the angrier I became.

The wind kicked up outside and the light from the utility pole had to pass through a tree in the neighbor's yard. The jostling leaves caused the light to flicker and break into numerous beams each bouncing off the ice in the *beczka* reflecting like tiny white pinpoint Christmas tree lights.

I remembered loading the bottles and my stinging hands and felt a weight in my chest. I heard my father's words "good job" and saw his face when I remained silent. Not so good a job. Not so good at all.

I became possessed by the pressure of shame and failure and wanted to punish someone. Certainly, not my father. He'd said I'd done a good job. Punish myself? For what exactly? Punish the backyard for not being different? That was silly if not stupid. I felt strung out, like the wire between the two clothes poles, and I didn't know what I was doing there.

Out in the yard, in the corner opposite the tree that had earlier filtered the light, I saw the statue of the Blessed Virgin Mary that Anna had insisted on putting in the yard. The statue, known as the Kingdom of Mary, showed Mary standing on top of a half-globe with twelve gold stars scattered across its blue surface and a black crushed serpent beneath her feet. Dressed in a plain white dress trimmed in blue that fell freely to her feet, cinched with a gold and black braid just above her waist, and a white veil that covered her head, she held her arms open with palms facing forward, a gesture of blessing and acceptance. The statue sat atop a red brick pedestal my father had built for which he received scant appreciation from Anna who'd seen it as his obligation to perform and was blind to his craftsmanship and diligence.

To Mary's left a plain brown wooden cross stood, anchored in the ground, memorializing Antoni's death. His body had been interred in a proper burial at Saint Hedwig's cemetery but, despite Anna's objections, The Brothers wanted to place the cross in the yard to help keep the memory of Antoni alive. They respected their father and had liked him as a man. He almost never demanded of them nor criticized them. He appreciated what they'd done, especially the oldest three, to help him situate the family in the New World. Anna argued that Antoni was not a saint, and he most certainly did not match the status of the Blessed Virgin but The Brothers insisted and Anna relented on the condition that the cross not be white, because white was the color of purity.

Whatever his faults, when it came to his job Antoni could be trusted: a stable and dependable worker who trudged to the Ford Motor plant every day regardless of the weather, completed his job, a job that would be exactly the same the next day and every day, day after day. Most days, before returning home, he would stop at the local tavern to "put away a few." That was his life's ritual: trudge to work, do his job, put away a few, have beef bone soup with potatoes and carrots and rye bread and butter for dinner, then go to sleep. He was praised for being uncomplaining but was chastised by Anna for being virtually mute around the house.

Surprisingly Antoni and Aleksandr, the man next door, were friends. They were from the same part of Poland and had emigrated within two months of one another. Together they felt a sense of rootedness, like brothers, a sense of identity they understood and even after thirty-plus years in Detroit still longed for.

On Saturdays, they secluded themselves in Aleksandr's dirt floor, backyard barn, a structure and a memory that umbilically connected both of them to the Old Country. They had dug a small hole in the dirt so they could play "Washers," a simple game consisting of round, metal, silver-dollar sized industrial washers with a dime-sized hole in the middle. Sitting on low stools at a carefully measured eight feet away, which was just a fraction larger than the washers, they pitched the washers into the hole. They'd devised simple rules: five points when the washer landed flat on the bottom of the hole and had not touched the lip or sides as it fell in; four points if it touched the lip or sides on its way into the hole but laid flat at the bottom; three points if the washer leaned up against the side wall nearest them; two points if the washer leaned up against the side wall furthest from them, because for some reason they believed that was an easier toss to make; two points if the washer did not fall into the hole but hung on its lip and could be purposely knocked in, but that shot had to be announced beforehand; and one point for each washer that had not fallen into the hole but was nearer to it than its opponent. To hear them laugh and shout and argue and measure the distance from the side of a washer to the lip of the hole within a sixteenth, or thirty-second, and even a sixty-fourth of an inch made the neighbors laugh and wonder if Antoni and Aleksandr thought they were in some kind of international competition. They never thought that. It was the Old Country brotherhood and belonging they craved and enjoyed.

I'd been invited into the barn once so they could show me the game. I wasn't yet six and to this day I can still feel the honor and privilege I felt entering their inner sanctum. It must have been Antoni's doing.

I don't remember much about Antoni. He didn't read. He didn't laugh, dance, or chit chat. But he did drink.

One summer afternoon, I was playing in the back yard when I heard screaming in the alley. *Busia* Anna came running toward the house her eyes literally bulging in terror.

Behind her Antoni ran waving his fist in the air. My mother, who was pulling weeds in the flower bed along the back fence, heard the noise and leaped up just as Anna reached the back gate. In her panic, Anna couldn't get the gate open, which panicked her even more. When she finally did open it, she ran past my mother, her arms flailing, shouting, "He's going to kill me," and disappeared into the house.

Anna had become fed up with Antoni's drinking at the local bar and decided she would put a stop to it. She prayed for guidance and God spoke to her telling her she was in the right and Antoni would comply. So she mustered her courage, strode to the bar, opened the door, and burst in on the men.

"Antoni," she snapped, "*przestać pić i iść do domu*" (stop drinking now and go home). She stood in her full height because she had God on her side.

Stunned, Antoni couldn't believe his ears. She dared invade his place of retreat and relief, his domain of men?

His friends were stunned as well, but they quickly recovered. "What? Are you without words?"

Antoni's mind had frozen.

One of the other men began a taunt, feigning a woman's voice. "*Iść domu, teraz, Antoni. Iść domu.*" (Go home now, Antoni. Go home). Some of the other men erupted in laughter and their insults snapped him out of his daze.

Humiliation surged through his blood and bone, humiliation that could not and would not be born, and surely not in front of his bar buddies.

It was then that Anna realized she'd made a mistake. God was wrong. She'd been abandoned. She could feel Antoni's rage from across the room and she turned and bolted out the door. Antoni didn't move until several men started up the taunt again, "*Iść domu, teraz, Antoni. Iść domu.*"

Antoni threw down his shot of Seagram's and flew out the door.

As he burst through the gate, my mother tried to stop him but he knocked her up against the fence between our house and Uncle Julli's next door and she fell to the ground before he slammed the back door vanishing into the house. I had never seen anything like that and we could still hear the ruckus inside.

"Stay here," my mother commanded me as she got up and rushed into the house.

Anna had tried to flee through the front door but it was locked and she couldn't manage it before Antoni charged her and threw her onto the front room couch, pinning her with one knee buried into her chest.

He raged, "Go home now? Now?" raising his fist to punch her in the face.

My mother screamed, "You stop that! Stop! What are you doing, Antoni?" and broke the rush of his rage.

He stopped mid-air, befuddled. She'd never called him Antoni before, always Papa. Lowering his fist, he growled menacingly, "Get out, Helena."

"*Co robisz*, Antoni? What are you doing?" my mother demanded.

"*On mnie zabije*," (he's going to kill me), Anna wailed.

"*Jeb się, glupia kurow*," (Fuck you, stupid bitch), Antoni pressed his knee harder. "*Przy znajomych cholero, przy moich znajomych*" (In front of my friends? God damn it! In front of my friends?).

Anna screamed, "*Boże chroń mnie, on mnie zabije*" (God protect me, he's going to kill me). Anna loved high drama and used it to her advantage, but that afternoon she wasn't sure. After decades of her disappointment with and disapproval of him, which she was never able to hide on her face or in her body, might he now kill her?

"*Zobaczysz, jak się nie zamkniesz*" (I will if you don't shut up).

"*Co ty mówisz*," my mother shouted. "What are you saying?"

"*Ostrzegam cię*, Helena," (I warn you, Helena, get out).

Anna moaned. She was having trouble breathing.

My mother crossed the room and stood face to face with her father. She grabbed him by the shirt. "*Stój, psia kreff, stój.* Stop, God damn it, stop." Her ferocity flooded the room. The expression "God damn it" burned in her mouth. She had never been that fierce with anyone. She couldn't help witnessing her strength, resolve, and authority: but she was also frightened by her eruption.

Just as brutally as it all began Antoni whipped his knee out of Anna's chest spitting, "*Sucha stary suka,*" (dry old bitch), and walked back through the house and into the basement.

Anna moaned as my mother sat next to her on the couch.

"Are you okay?" my mother asked.

"He is a mad man," Anna sputtered in Polish, "out of his mind. You saw! You saw."

My mother merely nodded. Even though Antoni had his fist raised, my mother never believed he'd have followed through. She'd never told Anna but she felt sorry for Antoni, for the soul-crushing drudgery he'd endured every day to keep the family afloat. Except for the threat of hitting, my mother agreed with Antoni.

When I came in I could hear Antoni roaring in the basement: glass breaking, wood splintering; violent cursing in his native tongue.

The next day, when I asked my mother what had happened, she looked at me with the *wielkem*, the bad eye, as it was known in my family, and I knew better than to pursue the question. It wasn't until years later that she told me the story and how, after that day, Anna and Antoni grew fatally estranged.

Two years later, Antoni was diagnosed with lung and stomach cancer brought on by the relentlessly toxic conditions inside the Ford foundry. He'd been complaining about pain, but only to my father, and then minimally, so my father felt no alarm. Seven days after the diagnosis Antoni died. He was fifty-four.

Because God Loves Us

The basement door opened with a short, sharp *SNAP*. It was tight and stuck at the top between the frame and the jamb. My father knew about that defect and curiously never got around to sanding away the flaw.

Uncle Ari popped around the corner and smiled when he saw me. "Jimush, *yak tam?*" He stayed at the door with one foot on the first step.

"I'm okay Uncle Ari."

"Good. Bring down three Strohs, would'ja?"

"Okay."

"Thanks," as he disappeared into the basement leaving behind the complaining door.

During World War II Uncle Ari served as a Navy Lieutenant flying F4U Corsair fighter aircraft. During his training at Grosse Isle Naval Training base just outside of Detroit, he would let everyone in the family know, which then spread to everyone on our block, that he was going to buzz our house at a certain time, usually on Saturday morning. The whole block waited in anticipation. At the precise hour Ari would fly low over our house, low enough that we could see his face. He'd flap the wings from side to side saying, "Hello." Everyone cheered and waved American flags.

Ari's long-time dream had been to become a doctor, an obstetrician—the only one of The Brothers and the only male on the block who had so rarified an ambition—and after the war he knew he could go to school on the G.I. Bill. When he made his dream known to his wife Blanche and her mother Henryka her mother exploded into wild-eyed, screaming scorn: "School? School? Are you crazy? You're a married man." She pointed to Blanche's belly. "Now you got a baby coming. You need to work." Ari turned to Blanche who had been so cowed by her mother all she could do was lower her eyes.

"A father, Blanka?" he asked.

Blanche nodded.

"You think like a boy," Henryka erupted again with even less control, "head in the sky." She grabbed Blanche by the hand and pulled her with such force that Blanche stumbled but said nothing. Henryka pointed again at Blanche's womb, shouting, "This. You see this. This is your doing. You and your thing. Now you want to go to school? You have a family. School is for children. Now you need to work."

Ari looked to Blanche. Shame forced her to turn away.

The closest Ari came to being an obstetrician was pacing in the waiting room during the birth of his first child. Instead of the university, he got a job in one of the Chevrolet factories where he remained until he retired.

I pulled three bottles out of the *beczka*, each one cold and dripping wet. My hands were too small to hold them securely so I pressed them against my chest. Icy wetness pierced through my shirt to my chest and I almost dropped the bottles before I could set them down on the landing.

Could I go into the basement with a wet shirt? What would I tell them if they asked? That I wasn't big enough to bring the three beers I'd promised?

I thought of picking up the bottles again but I knew I wouldn't be able to grip them. So I placed them, one at a time, on the first step down toward the basement and moved to the basement door where I could still reach back to get them. I knew the door was jammed, and if I pushed it open, which was the only way it would open, there I'd be in plain sight with a wet shirt and bottles lined up on the stairs. Why wasn't I bigger?

I brought the bottles, one at a time, down to the step at the door, but I was confronted again with the problem of lifting them all at once. There was nothing on the back porch, not a bag or a basket I could use to carry all the bottles simultaneously because my mother had "straightened out the porch." Straightening out to her meant clearing it entirely of whatever had been there, leaving only the *beczka*, "To make the porch nice for the party," an obsessive ritual she'd become consumed by every time relatives were expected. But nobody cared about the back porch, including my father. It was the back porch. That's all, the back porch. A drop spot. We came in and we dropped things. It was the catch-all where we put things when we couldn't figure out where else to put them. That's all. Except for my mother. She cared. It meant something to her.

I flushed with anger and confusion. 'Why does she do that? Who cares?'

My father had made a storage locker for my mother under the upper part of the back porch to store her yard and gardening tools. She could access it through a door on the outside of the house. I shot up the steps, through the outside door, and threw open the locker door. Looking inside I realized I'd made a mistake. What would I do, carry three bottles in a bucket large enough for eight or ten, or use the grass catcher from the back of the push lawn mower, large enough to hold an entire case? What was I thinking?

I was rushed with panic because of my stupid idea, made worse when I remembered the bottles I'd left on the step at the basement door. If any of the men were to come through that door, not see the bottles, kick one, and break it, I would have my father's upper lip and who knows what else to contend with. So I charged back inside, picked up the cold wet bottles, all three together, banged against the door butt first and heard the *SNAP* as it flew open. The force I'd exerted to push the door open caused me to almost fall backwards into the basement.

As I stumbled in, a horrifying image flashed of me falling down, face first, the bottles breaking underneath me, my bleeding all over everywhere, and the party coming to a desperate halt. 'Oh God, please don't let that happen.'

With an act of equally desperate will I caught my balance, straightened up, bottles intact, and turned to see how the men were responding. I expected laughter from the men and my father's lip.

But they hadn't noticed.

I couldn't believe it.

Hadn't they seen me stumble in backwards? Hadn't they heard the bottles clink as I strained to catch my balance? No they hadn't. They were braying and bellowing, slamming cards on the table with more and more force.

They saw nothing.

Suddenly a stinging flared up inside me, a thousand thousand sting points all at once, and I imagined bees, or nettles, or thorns had come alive inside my skin. I'd never experienced such a feeling before, like pins pushing into me, and after every prick they'd move to some other spot.

I was burning and they just kept playing, not looking up. I'd been attacked and they kept shouting and swearing. I was in trouble and they didn't know.

Then a stunning realization—I could be invisible. No matter what I did I couldn't be seen. Invisible.

After my distress with the bottles; the efforts I took to solve the problem of carrying them; my wet shirt and cold chest; the panic I felt imagining one of the men kicking and breaking a bottle splashing beer all over the steps; the cursing that would surely be heard in the basement and the dining room; the humiliating images of my bungling; my detestable hands that were too small. None of it mattered.

How was it possible?

The men kept slapping and smashing cards against the table. Their shouting and laughing became louder and louder, accentuating the prickling chaos inside of me, until their voices fused together into one unintelligible mass of sound like the hissing roar of a steam locomotive bearing down on me.

I shut my eyes with such pressure that my whole face rumpled in protection. In that instant, the roar stopped completely, as though the sound had been sucked away by a vacuum leaving a tangible, thick silence.

After what seemed like forever I opened my eyes. The piercing cold stabbed my chest and spread throughout my whole body until I shivered. The pricking stopped and I became aware of myself standing in the basement clutching the cold bottles against my chest.

All the men were now focused on me, puzzled, except for Uncle Ari who smiled, "Good boy, Jimush. Don't stand there, open them."

"Huh?"

"The beers. We can't drink 'em until they're open." Uncle Ari laughed.

"Open?" I stammered. My father's lip curled. "Where's the opener?"

Uncle Ari pointed, "On the clothes table."

"Oh. Okay."

"Bring 'em to me. I'll open 'em," my father barked.

"Let the kid do it, Eddie. He's gotta grow up." I loved Uncle Ari for supporting me but wished he hadn't. I remembered my father's "Good job" and didn't want to make any more mistakes. "Come on Jimush, you can do it."

My father turned to his cards which I took as either his permission or disinterest. Either way it seemed like I had to open the bottles.

As I moved to the table I heard Uncle Chez whisper, "He's just a kid, Eddie. Don't make it so hard." My father kept his eyes on his cards.

Half of our basement was allocated to work and storage. Laundry for the family regularly brought my mother, and sometimes Anna, down to the two concrete wash tubs with built-in scrubber boards and a Maytag Wringer Washing Machine. Rope lines for drying that were taken down for parties and special occasions stretched across the length of the work area, where the table stood for folding the dried and ironed clothes. The table was a permanent fixture.

A gas stove initially intended for vegetable canning and making fruit preserves stood near the floor to ceiling wooden cabinets packed year-round with wax-sealed Mason or Bell glass canning jars, a job my father took over and did like he did everything else with an eye to perfection

A coal-fired furnace dominated the other end of the work area. Just beyond it, the coal bin: an 8x8x8 room used exclusively to store coal which was delivered as needed and fed into the bin through a metal door on the side of the house under the front room window. An inner plywood wall had been constructed in the room, eighteen inches from the main door, which kept the coal from spilling into the basement proper. A sliding gate in the wall permitted us access to small amounts of coal we then shoveled into a bucket and took to feed the furnace.

From his truck in the street the man who delivered the coal would set up a metal, semi-circular mechanized chute with an embedded conveyer belt down our walkway and, making a right angle, enter the coal bin. He would stand in the bed of his truck and shovel coal into the chute, creating a stream of coal pouring through the bin door. The first delivery would arrive toward the middle of November and I took great pleasure in standing beside the chute watching the coal disappear into the bin. When the delivery was complete the bin behind the plywood wall would be full from floor to ceiling.

We spent a lot of time in the basement as a living space because it was warm in the winter and cool in the summer. Pots of beef or chicken soup rose to a boil and then simmered, filling the basement with rich aromas of comfort and wonder. I looked forward to chicken soup with carrots, celery, and my mother's homemade noodles, anticipating the gizzard and heart which were my favorite pieces.

Neighbors three doors away had a small chicken coop in their backyard and I spent time watching and talking to their chickens. Sometimes I wondered if the heart I was eating belonged to one of the chickens I knew. I asked my mother and she assured me that all of the chickens we ate were purchased either from the corner grocer or from the poultry yard six blocks away. I was relieved—but never completely.

My mother had cleared the clothes-folding table when she "straightened up" for the party and dialed in the radio to the station for the Tigers game against the Yankees so the men wouldn't have to search for it. She'd also left an empty Strohs case, a repository for the empties throughout the night. My father hated when empties were left around the house. "What do they do at home," he'd snarl, "shit in their own beds?" Everyone knew—especially Julli—that all empties, what the men called "dead soldiers," had to be placed in the case. I could already see nine empties—four that had been brought down from upstairs and five more the men had finished in the fight and fury of their pinochle wars.

I saw the church key next to the beer case, a four-inch piece of metal with a triangular tip for punching holes in cans at one end and a rounded tip with a small hook for prying open bottle caps at the other. My uncles relished calling it a churchkey. It opened more delight and meaning for them than anything that happened on Sunday morning.

As I reached the table, knowing the men were watching, especially my father who had looked up from his cards, my concern with the three bottles I was clutching rose up again. How do I set them down? Rather than wrestle with them, I bent over and was able to set them down all at once. My decision had been the right one. Good job.

I grabbed the first one by its neck and clumsily placed the churchkey against the cap. I'd seen it used by the men but had never opened a bottle myself. My first attempt failed and Uncle Chez said, "That's okay Jimmy." I turned to him.

He was seated next to my father. "First times are always tricky."

My father stared. It felt like he was testing me, waiting to see if I would pass.

I looked at the opener and could see that the rounded end had to be placed on top of the bottle cap and the hook under the edge of the cap. I set it and gave a tug. The cap popped right off. Chez cheered, "That's it kid. That's the way."

"Good job, Jimush," Ari clapped, "now open the rest." I wished Ari had not said "good job."

My father looked back into his hand. Years later I realized that my father lived with a burning and almost constant sense of humiliation; a product of his father Louie's belittling contempt and crushing rage. My father's life was a constant project of protecting against embarrassment and disgrace. Once it became clear that I could handle the bottle-opening, the men returned to their pinochle.

In the other half of the basement, the side that my family used as a living and play space, the men sat on white wooden straight back chairs around a red and white porcelain-topped table that had once been the kitchen set. Julli and Chez sat saddle style so they could balance on the rear legs and rock back and forth as they contemplated their next move. Once decided they would surge forward, crashing the front legs to the concrete floor, and slam a card against the table. That simple action gave them a sense of authority—what they had little of in their lives.

Four men played the round and two watched. Partners were determined as each man drew a card. The men who drew the highest two cards were partners and the same for next highest two. The men with the lowest ranking cards had to sit out the round and watch.

My father and Julli were partnered against Bo and Chez. My father was not pleased. Julli scowled appropriately making certain not to lose face, but inside he hoped he would play well to impress my father who possessed very little patience for Julli's lack of impulse control, which rarely produced a "best outcome," whether in home repair or pinochle. So Julli was sure to have an open Strohs handy at all times.

Jerry and Ari played the role of kibitzers, offering unsolicited and at times unwanted advice. Although the suggestions or corrections from the kibitzers could lead to explosions, kibitzing was as much a part of the evening as the game itself. When one of the teams reached two-hundred and fifty points they won the round and remained at the table as the losers changed places with the kibitzers so everybody had a chance to play.

The men never played for money: just pride and power.

As I delivered the beers I tried to catch my father's eye but it was his turn to deal. He shuffled the cards making certain there was not the slightest inelegant move as he cut the deck in two, riffled the cards together so that only the tips touched and then forced them into an arc. When he released the pressure the cards fluttered down beneath his hands reforming the stacked deck, and he smiled, surveying the table to be sure that everyone had witnessed his shuffling skill. My father tended to undermine his stature with the haughty pride he took in such small triumphs.

I hung around the table watching the game, taking cues for how I might play when they let me.

"There, God damn it," Chez blared, slamming down a card.

Julli and Bo played their cards in order. My father was last to play. He coolly stared at Chez and laid down a trump card to win the hand.

"Fuck," Chez yapped. "I thought I had it."

"I knew you didn't," my father smiled.

"That's it, Ketchup," Julli laughed. "Good job."

My father tilted his head back, obviously pleased with himself.

"You shit, Eddie," Jerry chastised my father. "You know, sometimes I think you'd'a been really good in the infantry stabbin' guys with a bayonet."

"Hey Jerry," Julli shot back, "when he's right he's right and right now he's right."

"You know fuckin' well, Julli, I wasn't talkin' about the hand."

"Enough,' Bo ordered, "It's my deal." The bickering stopped as Bo quietly picked up the cards and shuffled.

Bo held the position of overseer in the group, a kind of governor who knew when to step in and stop things. He'd gained his authority not because of any special training he'd had but because the men accepted that about him. It was the way he carried himself—contained and to the point—and whenever he spoke it seemed clear his voice was necessary.

My mother told me that Bo had shared with her the trouble he saw Julli get into as a child and the pain it caused Antoni and Anna. So Bo chose to be quiet. He became an observer and a commentator. He had the strength to step in, with timing that was nearly flawless, and his advice was sound, so they decided he must be wise.

Later in his life Bo joined the Knights of Columbus, or the K of C, as we called it, and advanced to the Fourth Degree, the highest degree of membership possible. He purchased and proudly wore the formal dress of the Fourth Degree, a black tuxedo, baldric and sword, white gloves, cape, and a plumed naval chapeau. The more he became immersed in the K of C the less he frequented family gatherings, but, like all of The Brothers, he was never able to sever his ties with our house and Anna.

The cards having been dealt, the men started in on another hand and, as usual, their focus was intense. Knowing almost nothing about pinochle I hung around the edges of the table, watching. They paid me little mind. Even when I stepped in closer and placed my hands on the corner of the table, which I purposely did to see what would happen, they continued their growling, snarling, and slamming until the hand was done. Right then Julli startled me by reaching across the table and setting his empty Strohs between my hands. "Hey Jimush, get me another beer."

I was delighted to be the bartender since I'd just proved I could open the bottles, but then I saw my father glaring at Julli.

"What?" Julli snapped.

"Get your own beer."

"Oh, for Christ's sake Eddie get the stick out of your ass. He can do it."

Menace flooded the room in an instant. Even though he was on my side, I hated Uncle Julli for what he'd said. I wanted my father to get up and punch him in the face. I also felt it was all my fault. Why did I put my hands on the table? Why did I need to hang around? Did I really want to be with the men?

My father and Julli were locked in a stare-down until Bo whispered, "Eddie."

My father looked to him and Bo simply shook his head. My father backed down. There had been many times when Bo had been my father's defender and my father loved him for that, to the degree that my father was capable of love.

I could feel the danger beginning to dissolve. Placing the empty bottle in front of Julli my father turned to me and said, "Go upstairs and watch the women play."

"Can he get me my beer first?" Julli was neither challenging nor testing, but blurting.

"Go upstairs, Jim. Now."

"Come on, Jimush," Uncle Ari put his arm around my shoulder," I gotta take a leak. I'll use the pisser upstairs."

My father looked down at the table. I didn't know if I should be proud of him or feel sorry for him, but, mostly, I didn't know what to do. Ari gave me a slight push to place me in front of him and we walked to the basement door.

I heard the door *SNAP* shut as we headed upstairs.

"I'm gonna go outside," I said to Uncle Ari at the outside door.

"You sure?"

"Yeah."

"Okay," he said. "Don't let that shit downstairs bother you. Okay?"

"Okay."

Ari went up the stairs and into the kitchen and I stepped into the yard.

The moonless night seemed darker than usual: a thick darkness I thought I could feel. I reached out to touch it and my hand simply floated through the warm air. I expected it to be velvety smooth like the midnight blue on the vest that was part of my mother's ethnic Polish folk costume.

It had been sent years before as a gift from relatives in Poland but she never wore it, not even to Polish events. Her concern for what others might say kept the costume neatly packed in the crumpled cardboard box in which it arrived covered with thirty-three Polish stamps. I felt sad for her. I'd seen the delight in her eyes when she took it out and held it and how she looked up and far away toward something unavailable to me. And how she accepted what she was seeing as unavailable to her so she'd neatly repack the costume back into the box. Later I asked, but she couldn't tell me what she'd felt or thought or imagined. To this day, I have no idea what went on inside of her. I don't think she did either.

The grass, still wet from the watering my father had given it that afternoon, faintly glistened under the light from the utility pole. My father had taken over the lawn watering because he didn't think my mother had been careful or consistent enough to do a thorough job. She happily passed it to him because, truthfully, when she watered she'd become bored; sometimes the lawn received enough water and at other times hardly any.

Feelings about my mother and father rolled through me leaving behind a wake of confusion, a kind of haze like a barrier that made them seem so different from each other and me. The love I felt for them was what I now know to have been a mix of compassion and pity. They didn't know what to do or how to be with each other and they certainly didn't know what to do with me, so we all lived in a vague, gauzy estrangement.

I stood for a moment in the grip of those unshaped feelings finally deciding to go to the front of the house. As I made my way down the concrete walkway between our house and Uncle Julli's they subsided somewhat.

The street was quiet which added to the darkness, because the houses, including ours, were too old to have been equipped with porch lights. Still in the wake of what happened at the pinochle table I decided to lay down on the vinyl cushioned aluminum glider on the front porch. It had arms that flared out at a 45-degree angle which made sleeping very comfortable. During hot summer nights, I would sleep on the glider as a respite from my bedroom with the crucifix. For this night, it felt good not to be responsible for holding my body up. I felt good being alone, not having to deal with anybody.

My eyelids gently fell as I let the glider carry my weight and listened for the wingbeats of bats that hunted over our street. They roosted in the large industrial buildings at the railroad a block and a half away and in the large pickling plant at the end of the street whose doors, large enough to allow gondola cars carrying unpickled steel rolls to be unloaded, were always open.

I wondered what it might be like to be a bat. And I wondered why I ended up a boy, not an ant or a fish or a girl.

The front door opened and Janice stood in the doorway. She could see I was stretched out full and there was no room for her but she asked anyway, "Can I sit on the glider?"

"Why did you come out here?" I growled but hadn't meant to.

"You don't want me to sit with you?" She was more curious than challenging.

Light from the front room glanced off her chest highlighting her knobby little breasts. When she had first arrived, I did want to touch her. Then I wanted contact. But now I was alone and that's the way I wanted it.

"Sure, if you want to," I said, surprising myself. As I sat up to give her space I wondered who said that, but knew it was me. "Wow," I mumbled.

"What?" she asked as she slid onto the far end of the glider bringing her feet up under her.

"Huh?"

"What did you say?"

"Say? Uh…I don't know. Nuthin' I guess."

"Oh. I thought you did."

"How did you know I was out here?"

"Through the window, I saw you come up the steps."

"Oh."

We were silent for about a minute.

"Do you like it out here?" Janice said.

"Uh huh."

"What do you like about it?"

"I like to look at the stars. Tonight there's no moon."

"Oh."

"Do you know that? There's no moon?"

"Uh…no, not really." Her blouse moved just a bit drawing my attention to her breasts.

"When there's no moon there's lots of stars."

"God made the stars," she said.

I wasn't sure what to say. I didn't know it then, but even though I had been a devout altar boy since kindergarten, something my mother dearly wanted, my connection to Catholicism was beginning to unravel.

"Do you know there are people who don't believe God made everything?" She spoke with an air of authority, the kind of authority available to the very young, the ignorant, or the true believers. I wondered where she got it from. "There's a girl on my block, her parents don't believe in God. I told her they are going to hell when they die. She started crying and ran into her house. The next day her mother told my mother and my mother told me never to say anything like that to anyone. I asked her why. She said 'Just because.' Aren't we supposed to tell everybody about God and heaven and confession?"

"Huh?"

"Aren't we supposed to tell everybody about God and heaven and confession?"

"I don't know."

"You should."

"What?"

"Tell everyone." Janice was annoyed with me.

"Why?"

"Don't you know anything? Because God loves us. And because Sister told us to."

"The Sisters at my school never told us that," I said competitively, not sure if that was the right thing for them to do or not, or for me to say.

"Really?" She was shocked, horrified.

"Uh huh." Pleased that I'd punctured her certainty, I smiled.

"What do they tell you?"

"About what?"

"About God."

In the first week of third grade at Queen of Angels Sister Mary Fulronette decided to teach us about eternity, but more to the point about how long it would be to spend eternity in hell. So she told us to be very quiet. As third graders we obeyed, completely. Then she told us to imagine the highest mountain in the world, higher than even the sky. Next, we were to imagine the smallest sparrow in the world, so small it could fit right in our hand. Then she told us to imagine that sparrow flying to the top of that mountain once every thousand years and removing one grain of dirt, so small you could hardly see it. She paused to intensify the drama, then finished with, "So, if you want to know how long eternity would be if you went to hell, when that sparrow takes away so much dirt that the mountain disappears, eternity would just be beginning."

"Our Sisters tell us about God all the time," Janice crowed, regaining her pride.

Her blouse shifted again and I wanted to touch her breasts, not her, her breasts. But I remembered that sparrow and suddenly worried that wanting to touch her breasts was a sin, and I couldn't get to confession until Monday during the daily mass we were compelled to attend, and if I died before then I would have a sin on my soul, and would end up in hell for eternity, way after that mountain disappeared. I turned away, looking for the stars and the bats.

Janice sat in silence for a few minutes and then got up. "They should tell you about God," she scornfully threw over her shoulder as she went back into the house.

I thought of stretching out again but didn't want my feet to touch the spot where she'd sat, so I moved to the top step of the porch and sat there.

Who was she to tell me what my Sisters should say? What business was that of hers? And who cares about God?

I couldn't get comfortable on my butt, shifting from one cheek to the other, and I couldn't get rid of the image of her face when she said, "Because God loves us." She made me feel guilty. Somehow, I was wrong. That's how she looked at me when I opened the door to leave the bathroom and she was there; like I'd done something wrong.

I noticed my right leg bouncing as though under its own decision. That was the first time, to my memory, I was aware of my agitation expressed through my frantic leg.

I tried to stop it by an act of will without success. So I held my leg down, first with one hand on my knee and then both hands. I felt the energy spring from my toes into my foot up into my calf. It seemed to explode into my knee driving my leg up as though the energy was desperate to escape. I watched my throbbing leg as though it belonged to someone else. I was angry. Really angry. When I realized how I felt I became even more angry. Janice. It was Janice. She made me angry. Really, really angry.

"God damn it," I muttered and was shocked. I'd never said that before. Never cursed. I'd wondered what it might be like to swear, but I never did. I thought about that sparrow again. Twice in one night. Two sins.

"God damn it" came out again. I was in the grip of something that might condemn me to hell.

I focused my attention, feeling the air around me, looking inside me, searching for any clue that God might have heard, that I might be condemned. Nothing. I sensed nothing. Maybe God hadn't heard. Maybe I was okay. But God hears everything. Sister Fulronette had said that, "If God stops thinking about you for even one second you would go out of existence." That hadn't happened. I was still alive, still in existence. I focused again, trying to detect something, anything that might let me know about my mortal soul. Nothing. Not a squeak. Not a peep. Nothing.

I'd been certain that if I ever swore something horrible would happen. Hellfire would explode and I would be swallowed. But nothing. Nothing. I was okay. Safe.

"God damn it," I tentatively whispered as a test just to be sure. Nothing. Again. Nothing.

My leg had stopped bouncing and I hadn't noticed until just then. A sign? I didn't know. Better than bouncing out of control.

I laid back on the porch. So many stars. More stars than I'd ever seen. I began to cry from relief. From relief of what? I wasn't sure. Maybe not ending up in hell. Maybe from my leg not bouncing. I wasn't sure.

The front door opened behind me. This time if it was Janice I wasn't going to let her sit next to me or near me. I was sure about that.

"Time to eat, Jimmy," my mother announced. "Come in."

I sucked in a deep breath of relief, glad it wasn't Janice.

"Okay Ma. In a minute." I wanted to look at the stars again.

"Be quick," she finished and disappeared into the house.

I stayed there for a moment longer then slowly got to my feet. As I turned to go in I saw the spot on the glider where Janice had been sitting. I felt anger again. When I grabbed the doorknob, I heard myself think, 'Who cares about God?'

Familiarity Breeds Contempt

All traditions have their rituals. Our family's Friday night pinochle and poker gatherings were built around the male and female card games. But another rite was also religiously observed: the feast—so much a part of the weekly gatherings that without it they would not have ended but they certainly would have lost a significant part of their appeal.

After an hour or so during the game my mother would leave the poker table and begin to lay out the feast. When the card party nights first began, the other women offered to help, but my mother consistently refused. "No, you go ahead and play," she insisted, "there's not that much to do." She appeared good natured and generous. Actually, she didn't like poker. She thought it led to jealousy and spite because the game offered the women the family-sanctioned opportunity to compete, but without the rules and protocols the men understood, so they could be cruel to each other during the evening. They didn't shout and swear like the men. Their gibes and taunts were subtle, perhaps not recognizable by a stranger, but their words were barbed nonetheless. My mother hated that the women were also prone to talk about each other away from the game and she didn't want to slip and give them any fodder to discredit her. Although not above gossip, she recognized its danger.

In the late summer between her seventh and eighth grade my mother shared with her then best friend, Anka, how she was attracted to Dariusz, a handsome boy in their class they called Dariu. She told Anka how she'd had a dream that Dariu thought she was beautiful; and how, in her dream, they encountered each other during the late afternoon at the end of the street where the alleyway began, and how he grabbed her and kissed her very gently on the mouth. My mother swooned and Dariu held her up with one arm. When she came out of her swoon he was looking down at her, his blue eyes penetrating to her very soul. The girls giggled in a combination of preadolescent shyness, delight, and sexual tension.

My mother's revelation was particularly powerful: to be sure because of its sexual content; but also because she had made herself so vulnerable in a neighborhood where that kind of dream demanded shame and an instant confession, and, even more frightening, a concern that the devil might have invaded her mind in the night and could be working to tempt her from her purity.

That fall, upon returning to school, and without my mother being present, Anka told Dariu about my mother's "sex dream." And to make things worse she told him in front of a group of other eighth grade girls. When the girls laughed, Dariu blushed, evoking even more and louder laughter which caused his face to flush into a darker and even more intense shade of red.

Just then my mother walked up and Dariu exploded in a rage. "I would never kiss you." His saliva sprayed across her face. At first her shock prevented her from realizing what was happening. She just stood, staring at him.

"Look at you," he snarled. "Look at you. Big stupid eyes. How could anyone want to kiss you?"

The other girls mocked her by pretending to swoon and moan. "Oh Dariu. Kiss me again, Dariu," followed by louder and more hurtful laughter.

As it became clear how her dream had been betrayed and that she was caught in a swirl of meanness and spite, she turned to Anka who was also laughing until she saw my mother's puzzled, questioning gaze. Anka immediately dropped her head and became silent. When she looked up the expression on my mother's face had turned from puzzlement to hurt and Anka could see the tears just breaking down onto her cheeks. Realizing the impact of her betrayal, Anka ran away, leaving behind the coarse and merciless laughter. Dariu pushed his way through the girls and fled. The fun over, the girls drifted away leaving my mother frozen to the spot.

In that moment, my mother decided she'd let herself become too close to Anka, shared too much with her, and worst of all, believed Anka could be trusted. It was wrong to let anyone other than Jesus see into your heart. In the intensity and finality of that pain she adopted a stance she later described as "Familiarity breeds contempt" and adhered to it for the rest of her life. So when she would say to the other women, "You go ahead and play, there's not that much to do," what seemed like generosity was largely mechanical. She knew to smile, even laugh, which served as her way of keeping familiarity at a distance without appearing distant. Although throughout she envied those whom she said "didn't care," she did care—to protect herself from "never ever letting that happen again." She never allowed herself to reveal her deepest yearnings to anyone and she never acted on them, until they atrophied and she was safe from desire.

The wall she'd built around herself, cemented with apprehension and mistrust, had paired with my father's stance of protecting against impotence and shame. The guard each of them maintained no longer arose as a reaction to the moment but had become part of their unconscious character structure, keeping them emotionally distant, bonding them together in a lock of mutual aversion. Her need to serve and defend The Brothers was the only expression of tenderness she permitted herself and even that was not without danger. The women teased her, accusing her of treating The Brothers like she would treat a lover, except, of course, for the sex. They were not astute enough to see that she'd pushed away her needs for closeness and connection for so long that she ceased recognizing what she was doing—giving what she wanted but could never get.

My mother set the table with cold cuts—pork baloney, hard salami, head cheese (not a cheese at all but made with the flesh from the head of a calf or a pig set in aspic and pickled with vinegar), and, of course, a selection of beef or pork *kiełbasa wiejska* (Polish country sausage). The meats were placed, or slapped as the men liked to say, between two slices of either rye or pumpernickel bread and slathered with a choice of homemade hot mustard or horseradish (a version with sour cream for the women to blunt the fire), hot pickled-peppers from my father's stock in the basement, and sliced tomatoes. Side salads of cucumbers in sour cream and vinegar, or potato with chopped egg in mayonnaise, and an ample supply of Better Made potato chips completed the feast. To drink, there was beer for the adults and red pop for Janice and me. My mother provided paper plates and after the men and women made their choices they spread out through the house to eat.

The eating done, the games would resume. At the close of the evening my mother served the second part of the feast, dessert, which was never called dessert: homemade apple pie and a variety of pastries purchased from the local Polish bakery. The adults drank coffee and Janice and I were given milk.

As I walked from the front porch into the house Uncle Jerry and Mary Therese were leaving. Jerry's self-opinion normally kept him away from the family, to such an extent that I'd forget about him and then be surprised when he appeared.

Of all The Brothers Jerry was the only one who lived in Dearborn. He owned a brick house with a built-in garage: made of yellow brick, the only one of its color on his block, he'd bought it for that reason. For the rest of the family who lived in the inner city, Dearborn, a quasi-suburb just west of Detroit, might as well have been Grosse Pointe, or the Chicago lakefront, or Beverly Hills. Considerably smaller than the wood frame houses we and the others lived in Jerry's home nevertheless gave him a leg up, a sense of superiority, a point of pride he relished.

I envied their brick house for its beauty and design. When we'd drive up I'd feel something special. Though I didn't have words for it, I appreciated its elegance and a sense of dignity, even though I felt cramped and confined in it during those rare instances when we visited.

As she passed me, Mary Therese smiled. "Good night, Jimmy." She opened her arms to hug me but I stiffened and forced a smile instead. She exuded a musty smell that I'd thought must have come from under her arms. Still my forced smile wasn't fair to her. She was never insincere and she never did me harm. But she reminded me of Anna and that alone was enough to keep me from wanting to be hugged.

When Jerry passed, he nodded, acknowledging my presence. As he opened and held the door for his wife who'd been waiting he shouted, "*Dobranoc.* Good night," and was gone without shutting the door. I resented him because he always treated us as though we were to cater to him.

No matter his status, however, he too could not sever his family connection completely. He showed up for the poker and pinochle evenings out of a compulsion he could neither understood nor control. The best he could do to maintain his sense of independence was to leave early.

On my way to shut the door I noticed Janice on the couch. She looked at me like I was a pathetic unbeliever: not someone she should be afraid of, but someone who was stupid not to know that God loves us.

She'd drawn her legs up under her without having removed her shoes. I was hurt by her lack of care for the couch and I stared at her. How could God love her? She's the stupid one. But when she looked up my trance was broken and all I could think to say was, "Aren't you gonna eat?"

"No."

"Why not?"

"I don't like that kind of food." Her nostrils flared as though some foul smell had suddenly invaded the room.

Violent punishing images flashed in my mind that scared me—scratching her face with a fork, forcing food down her throat, watching her vomit. I had to shake my head to stop them.

"What are you doing?" Janice asked sincerely.

"Uncle Jerry didn't shut the door," I said, covering my thoughts.

"So?"

"So!? You gotta shut the doors."

"I don't."

"I do," I answered, with self-satisfied superiority.

She shrugged and walked off to the back of the house.

"Why are you going to the kitchen?" I snapped. "I thought you don't like that food?"

"I don't," she said without breaking stride.

"But—"

"I want red pop." She didn't even look back. As the unbeliever, I wasn't deserving.

It took me a moment before I shut the door and headed toward the kitchen.

The poker game was wrapping up for the feast break.

"I just love High-Lo," Vi giggled. She'd won the high hand in a pot which had grown to ten dollars with all the betting, so Vi's share was seven dollars. "Not a bad pot, huh Van?" she smiled innocently.

"The night's not over, Vi," Van said, becoming aggressive, blatant and biting.

"Stop, Van," Blanche pleaded, organizing the cards and straightening out the yellow-flowered oilcloth, preparing the table for anyone to sit and eat.

Irene had already moved to the kitchen with Janice at her side. Janice filled her glass with red pop and took a long slow sip. As she slid past me on her way to the front room, her still wet red mustache glistened across her upper lip.

I was hungry and made a baloney sandwich on pumpernickel with mustard and a handful of potato chips. Then I noticed Janice had taken the last of the red pop. There was a bottle of orange pop in the refrigerator but I hated orange and I wouldn't drink it anyway to show Janice that I didn't have to. I filled my glass with milk and took the chair near the stove, a good spot to be out of the way but still in the kitchen.

Irene and Blanche busied themselves with selecting paper plates and napkins for themselves and their men. "How's your mother, Blanche?" Irene asked.

"Not good. Doctor says cancer will shut down her kidneys."

"I'm sorry, Blanche," my mother half-whispered, keeping her voice down out of respect for the dying.

"Well...you know...what can you do?" Blanche paled, already suffering the coming loss of her mother.

"Nothing," Irene consoled. "That's the hard part...the worst thing when my mother died. They made sure she didn't have pain...but I sure did."

"I don't know what I'm gonna do."

"Do? You go on, that's what," Irene blurted as though it was patently clear. "What else is there?"

"Ya, ya," Blanche sighed.

An uproar from the basement preceded the arrival of the men. The Tigers, in a tight race with New York for the lead in the American League, had beaten the despised Yankees and the men were charged with a sense of triumph and power. Detroit had split a two-game series with the Yankees at New York which made the win even sweeter. I appreciated their excitement, but I was curious why they took baseball so seriously. None of them had ever played at any level. Not one of them was athletic in any way. I never heard them talking about betting on the game. So what did it mean to them?

I'd asked once why they got so excited about the Tigers and they dismissed me as too young to understand. Maybe I was too young. After all, they were the adults so they were supposed to know.

Despite their sense of triumph, they were emotionally, financially, intellectually impotent. They'd been brought up to accept that the source of authority was located outside of them, so they were followers, docile and compliant men who barked and growled and raged and, in the end, were weak and ineffective. They knew how to work, obediently punching a time clock, in and out, training the nuns at Queen of Angels were charged with so that the motor city could continue its productive hum. The men would deny their impotence and might even fight with their fists to prove their strength, but never against an established authority.

"Goddamm Yankees," Chez could be heard coming up the steps. "We sure killed'em tonight."

The women, except for Vi, shook their heads or rolled their eyes in a powerlessness of their own, because they had neither the inspiration, nor the energy, nor the know-how to make a difference in the lives of their men and by association their own.

We were American peasants who were told we could do or be whatever we set our minds to without the internal resources to actually follow through. Any forceful show of personal ambition or resistance to authority was condemned as selfish, unwarranted, misguided, unpatriotic, or sinful. The men and women of my family, everyone in the neighborhood and the church, were capable of self-respect only in the context of deference and bent knees. Genuflection was a sign of a worthy self.

I took a bite out of my baloney sandwich and had a sip of milk.

Chez came through the doorway and sat at the kitchen table, a glowing cigarette held firmly between his yellow-brown fingers. As soon as he saw Vi he placed the tips of his forefinger and thumb into his mouth, covered them with spittle, pinched out the hot end of his cigarette, and tossed the extinguished butt into a trash can my mother kept in a corner. Irene's eyes flashed and she stared at him until Vi cooed.

"Hi honey," and moved behind his chair to rub his shoulders. Her public expressions of affection were tolerated by the family, but they would have preferred her keeping such behaviors to herself. "Did you win?"

"Nah. Eddie and Julli won the first round."

"But the Tigers won, huh? That's really good."

"You damn right. We killed'em tonight. How about you? How you doin'?"

"I'm doing really good."

Van scowled from across the room.

Ari appeared in the doorway and smiled. "What a great spread, Helch."

Blanche took Ari's compliment as a personal cut and turned away to arrange coffee cups that had been placed around the coffee maker on the side of the sink opposite the makeshift bar, cups that hardly needed arranging. My mother's table wasn't extraordinary: quite typical of what she and the other women did for poker and pinochle evenings, but not up to Blanche's efforts and how she extended herself when the gathering took place at her house. It wasn't a matter of Blanche competing with the other women. Her own chronic grinding sense of inadequacy and guilt gnawed at her like an acid corroding the underbelly of her value and esteem. When they were first together Ari did compliment her, generously and often, but his words were measured against the immobilizing inadequacy in her own mind and she inexorably ended up in the shortfall. After a while Ari became less and less complimentary, yet he always made a point of praising my mother's efforts.

He'd noticed his wife's reaction and to protect her from being exposed, he said, "Hey Blanche, can I make you a sandwich?" She half-turned, hurt registering on her face.

"*Keilbasa*," she answered, barely audible and turned back to the cups.

"On pumpernickel, with a tiny bit of horseradish. Your favorite. Coming up." Ari's extra cheeriness rang hollow.

Although their marriage was still playful, at least as playful as Ari could make it, a strain in the early stages of its malignancy had grown between them.

Ari had made a habit of dropping by our house on Saturday mornings, alone and unannounced, with a dozen donuts from the nearby Old-Country bakery. My mother would brew coffee and they would sit and talk. It was a comfortable and predictable relationship. My mother had effectively been his mother after Anna had given up the role and they had a close and intimate connection, one my mother loved and Ari trusted.

One Saturday he began: "Blanche is scared of her mother...you know...since she was a kid...she can't talk back...stand up...when I try...she stops me." Ari lowered his head in sadness and disbelief.

"Did you ever try talking with her mother?"

"Henryka? She's crazy. She said it was none of my business...that Blanche was her daughter and I should stay out of it. When I said 'Blanche is my wife,' she screamed like a god damn witch—"

"*Shh, shh, shh,*" my mother whispered hoping to quell his cursing.

"Like a fucking crazy witch...'What?' she said, 'you think I don't know? Why didn't you keep your thing in your pants? Because you're a man. That's why. You can't do anything else.' She was a maniac. Then she hit me...hard...with her fists...here," he pointed to the side of his head. "Did you ever see that woman's eyes? She's a devil."

"My God."

"I don't know what I'm gonna do." Ari's face was filled with pleading, hoping my mother could give him an answer.

Surprised and alarmed, my mother asked, "What are you saying?"

Ari stared back, his eyes hardened.

My mother whispered, "Divorce?" as though at the mere mention of the word they would be plunged into the gaping, frothing mouth of Satan himself.

"I don't know."

His non-answer frightened her even more.

"You can't. *Nie volno.*"

He stared at the floor, his breathing heavier.

"Ari, it's a mortal sin."

"Mortal sin my ass."

"Ari, *shh, shh*...don't say things like that."

"Why not?"

"The church, Ari...God's law...I don't know. Just please don't."

The punishment for divorce was excommunication, an outcome everyone feared.

"I love Blanche...but...I can't stand it that she won't speak up...stand up for herself. It's been years and she never does it."

"She never did."

"What?"

"She never did."

"What are you saying?"

"I thought you knew."

"Knew what?"

"That she never did."

"You knew?" his head snapped up.

My mother jerked back in her seat.

"You knew?" he pleaded, perceptibly hurt and angry. "Why didn't you tell me? Warn me."

"You never saw it?"

"Why didn't you tell me, Helen?" He rarely used her formal name.

"I thought you knew. People knew. We all thought you knew. You were in love. No one wanted to spoil..."

"You all knew and didn't—"

"What would I have said?"

"I don't know...something...anything."

"If I'd said anything, would you have believed me?" she became firm, protecting herself.

"I always listened to you, Helen."

"You were in love," a love my mother silently lived through by proxy.

"Helen..."

"No, Ari. I couldn't have stopped you. There was nothing I could have said, and you know it. So I prayed for the best."

"Prayed! Prayed?" Starkly fixed on the irremediable choice he'd made for his wife, his spirit opened and emptied, and on a breath that had little more power than a whisper, he said, "This is what your prayer got me?"

My mother, thrust face to face with Ari's heartbreak—her favorite "son" whom she'd abandoned and betrayed—felt a flash of anger. 'How can he blame me?' she thought. 'He was a grown man?'

To keep from exposing her feelings she turned away and then moved next to him, stroking his head like he was a child. Her internal judge and jury slammed down the gavel convicting her of gross selfishness and unforgivable cowardliness because she knew she had been afraid to warn Ari about the fear bordering on terror at the heart of Blanche's sense of self and how she could not be relied on to make a good wife. And there were also moments when she thought she could've been a better wife for Ari, and moments when she wanted to, but such a marriage was impossible, shameful, mortally sinful. They'd be exiled from their community. Her thoughts frightened her so she banished them as soon as they arose.

Overwhelmed by the raw truth of what she'd done she said, "Let's not talk about this anymore...okay? Ari...okay?"

Silence.

"And this will be between just you and me, okay Ari? Okay?"

Resignation flooded his body and he slumped. There was no way out and he knew it.

"Okay, Ari?" She needed his assent to redeem herself. "Okay?"

"Okay...okay, Helch."

"Just between us, okay?"

"You and me..."

"That's it, my darling child. Just between you and me. Okay. I love you Ari."

She stroked his head.

"Hey Van," Julli shouted as he was coming up the steps from the basement. "Did'j'a make me a samich?" He purposely mispronounced the word to make light of his demand.

As everyone turned to look at her, Van's face buckled. Caught between the insult of being treated like a servant for which she would have loved to tear him to pieces and her concern that if she resisted filling his order he might explode in front of the others, a public eruption she'd had to face in the past, she remained silent, remembering how, at the time she'd agreed to marry him she was well aware of his reputation for heavy drinking and violence. How could she have believed she would change him?

In the doorway Julli barked, "Be sure to put a lot of Eddie's peppers on it." His words were sloppy and slurred, his eyes red and deadened, he was drunk again.

She glared at him.

"What, momma?" he shot back. "I'm not asking for a shot and a beer. I'm asking for peppers." He spoke slowly and deliberately as though his request was terribly complex and she was feeble minded so he had to talk down to her. "That's not too hard to understand, is it?"

Van relented, stepping to the table to fill Julli's order. She grabbed a handful of peppers, smashed them onto a slice of rye, slapped a stack of hard salami and head cheese on top, tossed on the other slice of rye, and crushed it down.

"Christ, Van, it's just a sandwich." Julli smiled, satisfied his dominance was still in place. "You want to kill it or what?"

She held out the oversized sandwich and the juice from the peppers dripped onto the floor. My mother came dashing over with a dish towel.

"That's okay, Van, I'll get it," my mother reassured, as she squatted to wipe the spot.

Van, in a lock with her husband, hadn't noticed.

Chez poked Vi, "Come on honey, we'll eat later," and they both left the kitchen.

"Does my momma love me?" Julli held the sandwich over his head like a trophy. "Yes, she does." More juice dropped to the tired yellow linoleum floor.

"Julli," Van snapped, "you're dripping."

"Oh, Jesus. Sorry Helch." As he lowered the sandwich to stop the dripping it dripped even more.

"That's okay, Julli." My mother dropped to her knees to better drag her dish towel over the barely visible juice beads.

"Hey Helch, I'll help you." Ari took a napkin from the table and squatted next to my mother.

Julli put his sandwich on a paper plate, scooped onto it a handful of potato chips, turned at the door to look back over the kitchen scene as though to focus and clarify his thoughts, muttered "Fuck it," and, using the wall to brace himself, as he slowly made his way down toward the basement. The basement door opened with its *SNAP* and then slammed shut.

Irene, leaning against the refrigerator, shook her head. "*Tsk, tsk tsk.*"

Van stood at the table. She couldn't look at the others. When she stepped out onto the back porch she seemed to be following her husband. But when we heard the outside door open and close we all knew she was gone.

I thought someone would go after Van but no one did.

My mother took her towel back to the sink to rinse it out.

"Here you go, Blanche." Ari handed his wife the *kielbasa* sandwich.

"Ari, Jesus," she moaned, "Your hands were on the floor."

"Oh," Ari stuttered, caught off guard. He set the sandwich down on the sink/bar, ran water over his hands, dried them with a used dish towel, picked up the sandwich and extended it to her. "There. That's better."

"Thanks," Blanche whispered, her hurt subsiding. She filled a cup with coffee and headed toward the front room.

"Ari," Irene broke in, "why isn't Julli up here with us? Why is he alone in the basement?"

"He's not alone. Bo and Eddie are down there."

"Uh uh," Irene corrected. "I saw them walking to the front of the house."

Ari shrugged and followed Blanche.

"Jimmy, go downstairs and see if you're father's there," my mother ordered.

I felt kind of spooky going down to the basement. If Uncle Julli was there, I didn't want to be with him alone. Sometimes he could be nice and friendly, but most of the time he was mean, and I was susceptible to his manipulations, like the time he teased me about going to Five Lakes.

Neighbors, three doors down, had purchased a set of four log cabins at Five Lakes in Northern Michigan they'd rent out during the summer. I had been there once with my mother and father when I was seven and loved it.

One afternoon the next spring Julli shouted across the back fence: "Hey Jimmy, you going to Five Lakes this summer?"

I had no answer.

"We're goin' for sure. Yeah, me and Paul (his older son) and Ronny (his younger son) are gonna spend two weeks. We already have the cabin. Aren't you going?"

I had no idea if we were going. My father hadn't said anything. But I became very excited by the possibility.

"Why don't you ask Ketchup, see what he says?"

I waited anxiously the rest of the day for my father to get home from work. When his Chevy pulled up I ran to the car and waited for him to get out.

"Dad, are we going up north this summer?"

"What?"

"To Five Lakes? Are we going?"

My father walked past me and toward the back yard.

"Paul and Ronny are going...for two weeks...Uncle Julli told me to ask you."

My father stopped and looked at me. He was angry and I felt as if I'd done something wrong.

"No we're not...and Julli's not either." He continued on toward the back of the house.

"But he told me he was and wanted to know if I was going."

My father stopped, turned to me, placed his hand on my shoulder so I couldn't move, and said, "No you're not...we're not... he's not."

"He's not? But he said..."

"I'm telling you, he's not." My father continued into the house.

I wanted to go up north so badly. I didn't know who to believe. As I was standing next to one of the metal cross-shaped clothesline poles, Julli came out into his back yard.

"My father says you're not going up north." I wanted him to affirm that he was so I could make the argument to my father that we should go as well.

"We're not, huh?"

"My father said so."

"Hmm." His mouth slipped into a callous and bitter grin.

"But you said..."

"No I didn't."

"Yes, you did. You said, 'for sure you were.'"

"If your father says we're not, I guess we're not."

"But..." My eyes filled with tears. Julli looked away. I never knew if he couldn't stand to see the result of his cruelty or that he was finished and was on to whatever was next.

As I walked slowly down to the basement I could feel my insides shivering. Unable to predict how Julli might be or what he would do, I could only remind myself of his meanness. As I pushed against the basement door it *SNAPPED* open and Julli looked up, pressing a cold Strohs against the side of his head.

"What?" he asked, staring, his eyes focused but distant, a predator deciding whether to lunge or lay off.

"Where's Dad and Uncle Bo?"

"Do you see them?" He seemed to be probing for a weakness.

"No."

I felt a mix of anger for having to give the obvious answer and anxiety because I suddenly felt frighteningly alone. Not because only the two of us were in the basement. I felt like I had been cast into outer space, immersed in an alien environment without the slightest notion of who I was and what I could count on.

"Then they're not here, right?"

"I guess." I heard contempt in my answer, contempt for his cat-and-mouse question and contempt for my limp answer, and contempt laced with shame because of the tears that were threatening to become visible.

He kept moving the bottle from one side of his head to the other as if he was trying to decide what to do with me. He set the bottle down, rubbed his face, and focused back on me. After a moment's drunken staring he said, "What do you know?"

"What?" What was he doing? Was he setting a trap?

"You know nothing." He rubbed is face again. When he dropped his hands, he was surprised to see me still there. Something shifted in him because he softened and, almost like he was begging, he said, "Leave me alone."

"What?" I blurted, without intention or control.

"Just leave me alone," he whispered, covering his face with his hands and rubbing his eyes.

I didn't wait for more. I ran up to the kitchen and reported to my mother that Julli was in the basement and "he wants to be left alone."

People in the neighborhood and in the family knew that Julli had "a drinking problem." But his erratic behavior extended so far beyond drinking as a credible explanation that some of the old women on the block whispered that he might be possessed and the church should be enlisted to perform an exorcism and rid him of his demons.

One Julli story they told that especially frightened and convinced them of his surrender to the devil took place during a Sunday afternoon in his backyard.

Julli had been drinking more than his usual and by midafternoon his balance was impaired, forcing him to sit on the outside steps at the back of his house. Suffering from a headache which was the brutal and pitiless companion to his drinking, he rubbed his temples trying to ease the pain. If it were only the physical pain Julli would've had no problem because he had an unusually high tolerance for pain. It was the images of his life that pressed at him, thoughts and feelings he could not control of a life he described as a "no-chance life." No one in the family, the neighborhood, or the church had any grasp of what he was going through that would have led them to take Julli's "no-chance life" seriously. Instead they passed it off as nothing more than the alcohol talking. "After all," they reasoned, "he's okay when he's sober."

He tried to think of his "rail days," but the memories accused him of not having had the courage to stay on the road, which actually meant not having had the mental or emotional strength to keep from returning to Detroit, and that made him feel even more wretched. He would have continued spinning downward, which he'd done many times in his past, even on the road, until the pain became so great that he would pass out to escape it. But this time he felt something brush by his head, closely and rapidly, startling his eyes open and thrusting his sluggish mind into alertness. "What the hell!"

Two sparrows had flown past him and he watched them land on the top rail of the crosshatched chain link fence between his yard and ours.

When the fence was installed, Julli had two design options. The "Barb" design allowed for the fence wire that extended above the top rail to remain pointed and sharp as a means of a defense against intruders. But because the fence would stand only four feet high and because there were children in the family, some as young as five, he decided against the barbed version. It might be dangerous to the little ones and not much of a barrier to anyone who was serious about coming over the top.

He chose the "Knuckle" design instead. The wire that extended above the top rail of the fence was bent in half and pressed tight against its lower half fashioning a row of rounded peaks, each one resembling the middle knuckle of a forefinger bent forward. Julli loved the knuckle design for its safety and appearance, what he liked to call its aesthetic, a word he'd learned when one of the workmen used it as the fence was being installed.

"What does that word mean?" Julli asked.

"Means good looking," the workman answered.

"Aesthetic huh?"

"Yeah, aesthetic. Good word."

"Yeah," Julli smiled. "I'll use it."

But the Knuckle design also made it easy for the birds to perch on the top rail.

Birds were frequent visitors to his backyard because it was healthy and vibrant. Julli took great pride in the yard even though Van did most of the yard work. No matter, he saw it as his.

The yard was organized into four sections: one piece along the fence separating Julli's yard from his neighbor's on the other side; a stretch that marked the boundary between the yard and the alley; the third along the line between our yard and his; and finally a large section in the middle for the lawn. Composed of rich loamy soil nurturing vibrant deep green grass, small but lush flower gardens on either side, and a large display of various flowering plants and bushes along the back fence at the alley, his yard stood out among the neighboring back yards as indisputably the best, as though touched by a special hand.

Extending out from the house for nine feet and spanning from one yard to the other, a cement slab that Julli called his "patio" provided space for a three-person, wooden-slat glider; a lockable wooden box for gardening tools; a bracket attached to the cinder block foundation of the house used to wrap-around and store the garden hose.

Julli had laid the concrete slab himself and took pride in making that space as a gathering place for Van's family including their friends as well as he took responsibility for sweeping, washing, and keeping his patio clean.

As he watched, the first two sparrows landed on the section of the fence adjacent to the patio. Two more landed on the fence above the side garden next to our yard. The two birds over the slab began preening and the two over the garden puffed and shook out their feathers. Julli thought about their freedom. For him freedom didn't mean being able to come and go whenever he wanted. Freedom meant the absence of an inner voice, the relentless harping critic who wouldn't leave him alone, especially when he'd had too much to drink.

Suddenly one of the birds puffed up and excreted a large black and white dropping over the side garden. In itself, the blob of excrement was harmless, and might even be beneficial to the plant life: but Julli took it as a warning that the birds over his cement slab might, and probably would, do the same, befouling his prized patio, and that would be unacceptable.

So he let out a wordless roar intending to scare off the birds. The two over the side garden took flight immediately. But not the two over the slab.

His roar caught the attention of an Old Country woman who was using the alley as a shortcut to church for late-afternoon Vespers. She stopped, hid herself behind a utility pole, and watched.

Julli roared again scaring off one sparrow perched over the slab, but the last one persisted. It never crossed his mind to simply stand up and approach the fence, which would have sent the last sparrow packing. He thought his voice alone should have been enough to scare the last bird away. And to make it worse, the sparrow hopped up and, for a moment, looked like it might fly, but instead repositioned itself on the top rail with its backside to Julli.

Julli's own personal Star Chamber set up court in his head and immediately convened to accuse him: *'How could you be so stupid to let a fucking sparrow make a fool of you?'*

"I'm not a fool," Julli blurted aloud.

'No? Well that bird is still on the fence and you're shouting like a crazy man.'

"I'm not shouting and it's not crazy." Julli unconsciously swatted his hand in front of his face trying to quiet the voice.

'What do you know? That bird's got more brains than you do.'

Julli leapt to his feet, needing a second to balance himself, and another roar exploded from his befuddled soul determined to make the bird fly. And it did. But before it launched itself it puffed up and jettisoned a large excremental glob that Julli watched splat directly onto his beloved concrete patio.

'Looks like the bird shit right on your patio and there's nothin' you can do about it. You're dickless.'

The sparrow shook itself off, spread its wings, and lifted off, which the alcohol coursing through Julli's brain interpreted as the bird's final insult, *'Up yours, Julli.'*

He sputtered in rage and humiliation as he rushed and crashed into the fence, but the sparrow was long gone, leaving Julli to dismissal and disgrace.

He stood for a moment shaking his fist at the sparrow that was already out of sight, then swatting his hand across his face as though he felt the draft from the sparrow's wings.

'*What are you doing? That bird's two blocks away by now. God you are stupid.*'

Julli rushed into the house. Moments later he reappeared with a large flathead screwdriver, a pair of pliers, and ferociously attacked the fence, determined to bend up to a point each and every wire over the slab section to make it "fucking hard" for any more birds to befoul his patio. That was his plan.

In his crazed fit he imagined birds landing on that barbed part of the fence and impaling themselves on the sharp stiff pointed wire and couldn't help but laugh.

He jammed the screwdriver into the small space where the top half of the wire had been pressed close against the bottom half, and worked the screwdriver managing to create a larger spread. Next, he grabbed the upper half with his pliers and tried to bend it back into a point.

If he hadn't been drunk the job would have been much easier. But he was drunk and the fencing put up a powerful resistance.

But Julli was not about to be done in. He dashed back into the house and came back with a gasoline-fueled handheld blowtorch. He fired it up and focused the burner head on one set of bent wires enclosing them in very hot blue flame. He watched as the wire changed from hard silver to soft red and then grabbed it with his pliers and, even though drunk, he delicately bent it up into the point he wanted. With the blowtorch, it was easy. Once he knew he'd be able to complete the job he muttered, "I got you now, fuckin' birds."

He persisted, occasionally swatting his face against a draft that had long since dissipated, muttering about how he would not be insulted by "no god damn sparrow," periodically looking up to check the skies and waving his fist at possible incoming invaders, until that section of the fence alongside the patio was transformed into a spiked fortress twenty-seven barbs wide.

The old woman in the alley stared paralyzed in amazement and fear watching a man possessed.

When he stood back to look at his work he remembered the sparrow's splat on the concrete. In his frenzy, he'd stepped in it and made it larger by spreading it around. So, after a cascade of cursing, he unwound the hose, attached it to the outside spigot, and scoured the concrete as well as the bottom of his shoe.

Van, who'd been visiting her sister, returned to see Julli in a sweat. "What're you doing?"

Julli pointed to the fence and smiled. "No fuckin' sparrow ever shit on my patio again."

The old lady in the alley, who had long since missed Vespers, backed away until she was certain she was out of sight and ran.

Through the front room window Irene, who'd been looking for her husband, saw my father and Bo on the aluminum glider and called to my mother that she'd found them, gesturing the need for my mother to talk to them.

My mother opened the door and knocked on it to get their attention. When my father looked over she asked, "Ed, do you want anything to eat?"

"I'm not hungry."

"Bo?"

"Naw, nothing."

"What are you two doing here?"

"Nothing," my father said in a tone that meant 'don't ask any more questions.'

"Are you sure you don't want anything?" My father looked at her and she knew it was best she go back inside. As she turned she bumped into Irene.

"What's with them?" Irene asked.

My mother's eyes traveled an arc from left to right expressing her exasperation. "Who knows?"

As Irene made a move to go out to them my mother stepped in front of her.

"What are you stopping me for?"

"Just let them be."

"Why?"

"Irene..." she pleaded, "they don't want to be bothered."

"Bullshit, Helen," Irene flared, pushing her way past my mother. "Bo what the hell are you doing out here?" Bo, who was seated on the end of the glider nearest her, didn't look up. "Don't give me that you-won't-talk shit. Helen laid out the food. Now get in there and make yourself a sandwich or something." Bo still did not answer. "For Christ's sake, Bo, you gonna be a boy about this?"

"You know, Irene," Bo slowly and pointedly raised his eyes to meet hers, "you can be the biggest pain in the ass."

"Like I said, Bo, are you gonna be a boy about this or what?"

"Listen, Irene..." my father started.

"Don't give me any shit, Eddie. Unless my husband's become a baby, he can talk for himself."

"God damn it, Irene," Bo jumped in.

"Don't God damn me. Is this what you want? Disrespect your sister? Get your ass off that glider and get into the kitchen." Irene crossed her arms and waited. Had she been wearing a habit she would've looked just like one of the nuns at Queen of Angels. "Come on, let's go. Let's go."

My mother envied whatever Irene had inside that allowed her to be so strong.

Bo knew when Irene put her foot down there was little point in tangling with her unless he was prepared to go toe to toe. He had two options: go to the kitchen; or go to his car, call for Irene and Janice, and go home. But the consequences of the latter would go on for who knows how many days.

As he rose my father rose behind him and they both entered the front room on their way to the kitchen. Bo did not look at my mother who'd been standing just inside the doorway but my father glared as though she was responsible. Taking her cue from Irene, my mother glared back.

"Don't make it me, Ed," my mother hissed. My father ignored her by following Bo to the kitchen.

What some might describe as an irony, I saw as a simple fact. The men strutted and blustered imagining themselves as the dominant ones, at least when they were in each other's presence, but the women actually controlled the goings-on in all the separate families, each in her own style: Irene took charge, directly, face-to-face; Blanche could do no better than manipulate as a victim; Van loved the power and punishment of scorn and belittlement; my mother used resignation and withdrawal as her source of command. Vi did not consciously control. She had no need. Chez adored her and cheerfully did her bidding. Only passive Mary Therese appeared not to rule. She possessed a crack-the-whip memory and could recall details of events from years before, so people had to be careful around her.

Just as Bo reached the table and dutifully began to make a sandwich and my father poured a cup of coffee, a horrible scream shot through the house, a woman's panicked scream: a scream so unusual, so unexpected, so filled with terror that for a moment neither Bo nor my father could move, trying to determine where it was coming from. But then a second scream fixed its location somewhere in the back of the house. But who? A woman in the alley? Why? With a scream so intense serious violence had to be occurring. Rape? Murder?

My father tore past Bo, knocking his sandwich out of his hand and charged out the kitchen door.

What had been just the moment before a house of hushed anxiety erupted into a mass of electrified foreboding and a cacophony of stunned questions as everybody rushed to the back of the house.

"Did you hear that?"

"*Na miłość boska,*" (Mother of God).

"*Co do cholery?*" (What in hell?).

"Was it a dog?"

"Where's Van?"

"Is it Van?"

"Do we need the police?"

Julli, emerging from the basement, hollered, "What the fuck? Get out of my way," as he fell onto his knees at the outside door landing, stopping everyone cold.

"Somebody stand him up, he's drunk."

"Jesus, Julli, Jesus."

"Don't fucking yell at me," Julli threw a wild punch missing everybody. "Take your hands off me. God damn it, stop grabbing at me."

Ari got Julli to his feet as Chez opened the outside door. Julli bulled his way out into the yard with the others following like water from a collapsed dam: everyone but Blanche. She stayed inside looking through the porch window.

In the yard my father stood at the center of the lawn, frozen.

"What the hell's going on, Ketchup?" Julli had to clutch one of the wires stretched between the two clothes-poles to keep himself upright.

In the next yard, Aleksandr raised a leather belt and viciously brought it down across the shoulders of his daughter Agnes who he'd cornered against the back gate next to the barn.

Agnes screamed, then whimpered, turning away and covering her head with her arms.

Everyone in our yard stood petrified. Motionless. Barely breathing.

Coming out of the house I'd dashed toward my father and slipped on the grass landing near his feet. I'd never seen his face so red.

Aleksandr raised his belt again and whipped her, this time across her buttocks. The loose cloth at the seat of her trousers thwacked in response.

I could see Aleksandr's other daughter Zita covered in a worn and stained nightgown, standing against the back wall of their house smiling: a smile so sinister and malignant it sent a chill through me. She was enjoying the beating. I inched closer to my father.

Agnes screamed again and I could see Zita's smile widen and her eyes grow large.

"Eddie, do something," I heard my mother whisper.

Chez, Ari, my father, Bo, any one of them alone could have stopped Aleksandr, but a fierce almost savage territoriality dominated the minds of the men in our neighborhood so that property lines were sacred and never to be transgressed.

My grandparents and those of their generation had to claw and fight to establish their worth in a new world that hurled a relentless barrage of prejudice, denigration, and injustice they had to defy and overcome to hold themselves up in their own eyes—a self-esteem sometimes earned with blood and bone, others' and their own. They told stories of their ordeal again and again creating a powerful epic that curled around and seeped into every belief and expectation. Once they were recognized as here-to-stay and were granted entry into American society, elevating them into the lower class, they would permit nothing, nothing, NOTHING BY GOD to trespass on what they'd gained. A man's home was his castle and the fences containing it framed the precinct of his power and his being.

Furthermore, it was forbidden to interfere when a parent disciplined his child. No matter the form, no matter the brutality, no matter the appeal to the church, which would have condoned corporal punishment anyway, no one had the right or the sanction to intervene.

Agnes made a move to get away, but Aleksandr countered and kept her pinned against the barn. His chest heaved making room for short spikes of air he sucked in which barely reached his lungs before his chest collapsed blasting his breath out in a cry of unloosed savagery, a sound my father had heard before, a sound he'd kept locked in the deepest recesses of his memory, a memory which in that moment would not be denied, a denial my father had forgotten he'd even denied, the sound of his own father Louie who was no stranger to such sadistic rage.

For all the money and status Louie had amassed he would not spend any of it on his family. He said with a show of pride that he would not turn them into good-for-nothings. They had to work to pay for what they wanted, a glaring hypocrisy that didn't go unnoticed on the block or in the community. Despite his attempt to appear reasoned and righteous the more he preached the more the other men in the neighborhood "smelled bullshit stinking up every word."

But for Louie, what would be the point of spending on his family? That did nothing to enhance his prestige among the men. Even though he saw himself as a person of high rank and desperately clung to that imagining, he deeply craved membership the men denied him.

So he'd wait until he knew the local bar would be full and make a grand entrance, loudly announcing he was "buying a round for everybody." Or he would show up with more cigars than he thought necessary and hand them out to "everybody who wants a good smoke. Philadelphia Perfectos. Handmade."

Among themselves the men called him a *cienias*, a limp dick or loser. They hated him for thinking he could buy their favor and saw him as a hollow corpse. But they never turned down what he was giving away.

Because Louie was such a pinch fist with his family, my father, in the sixth grade, decided he would build his own bicycle by finding and assembling what he needed piece by piece, which he did. He scoured alleys, sneaked into junkyards, accepted parts from people who knew what he was doing, and he even earned the money to buy a part, until finally his bike was complete. Everyone called it "The Eddie." It served as a symbol of his independence, his determination, and his mechanical skill. He had no need to show it off. Riding it, and it rode very well, gave him evidence and the pleasure of what he had done and what he could do.

One day he was persuaded by some of the boys from the block to skip school and go off on a romp to the fields beside the railroad tracks, a persuasion that did not require much effort because school for my father was a painful bore. One of the guys had a pack of Camel cigarettes, and challenged everybody to "light up." Smoking was not uncommon among eleven-year-old boys in the neighborhood, but my father had never tried it. When he was slow to agree, one of the boys challenged him, "Hey Eddie, what're you, chicken shit?"

Even as a boy, my father took challenges, no matter how slight, as an assault on his character, and once provoked he would stand against the challenger whatever the cost. The boys knew that and wanted to see what he would do. He snatched the cigarette, lit it, and, to prove himself, he took a deep, first-ever drag that threw him into a paroxysm of convulsive, violent coughing as though he'd been attacked by a killer beast ripping through his chest as his whole body jerked and bucked to save itself.

The other boys fell to the ground laughing and taunting.

"Thought you was a big man, huh?"

"Careful Eddie, you'll cough your brains out your ass."

"Look at his eyes. Big as fucking silver dollars."

As he fought to regain control over a pair of lungs that would not be subdued, he heard the boys laughing and then become silent, their footsteps running away. He looked up and Louie stood over him, as cold and cruel as he'd ever seen him.

"*Do domu,*" Louie ordered.

His lungs still burning, my father had to march home with Louie behind him, doing his best to suppress his coughing.

When they got to the backyard Louie pointed to the chair he used when he sunned himself, ordered my father to sit, and then disappeared into the barn. When he reappeared, he carried a sledge hammer, rolling my father's bike into the middle of the yard.

"Skip school, huh? You think I'm stupid, huh? Think you can fuck with me, huh?"

With ferocious blows Louie smashed The Eddie reducing it to a mass of twisted and broken metal. With each blow a nightmare of shock and disbelief fused to keep my father seated. With every blow the small handlebar bell he'd purchased, what he cherished most on the bike, rang out, an alarm my father could not rise to answer.

Finally, my father's heartbreak and rage reached a pitch he couldn't control. He leaped from the chair and attacked Louie knocking him over. They wrestled for a moment, but my father's smaller size coupled with the desolation he felt watching his bike being demolished left him gutted. Louie pinned him, slapped him, punched him, dragged him to his feet by his hair, and pulled him toward the barn. From the back of the barn door Louie grabbed what he called the *Ruski pas*, a twelve-inch section of a barber's strap sliced into five ten-inch strips with the remaining two-inch base nailed onto the end of a foot-long piece of broom handle resulting in a formidable whip. He yanked my father back out toward the bike and began to thrash him anywhere the strap would land.

My father resisted until he fell to the ground, his energy spent, his will collapsed, the shock of what his father had done searing through his eleven-year-old mind. Louie continued the whipping, striking repeatedly until he was spent. He staggered into the house leaving my father in a heap of blood: his shirt, his trousers, his face and hands bloodied dark red.

"I'll teach you, you cheap whore," Aleksandr screamed as Agnes' knees buckled and she slumped.

He raised his belt again and Agnes curled into a ball. Before he could land another blow my father burst toward the fence, cleared it in one bound, grabbed the belt, wrenching it out of Aleksandr's hand. My father's yank threw Alaxendr off balance so he had to grab the fence to stop from falling, the belt buckle cutting a gash in the crazed man's palm.

Julli, still hanging from the clothes wire shouted, "Kill'im, Ketchup," with such force that he swayed backward and had to clutch on to the second clothes wire to stop himself from falling. "Kill that son-of-a-bitch."

Julli had never had any trouble with Aleksandr, no particular confrontation to want him dead. That mattered little because Julli wanted most things dead, especially himself.

Van, who'd stepped out of her house when the screaming began, and, as usual, was not noticed, took a melancholy delight in watching the whole scene, particularly Aleksandr's holy righteousness being exposed for the corruption at its source, and was disgusted with not merely his hypocrisy but with what she saw as the brutality at the heart of all religions. And to crown it off there was Julli, her alcoholic man-child husband, howling drunk, hanging from the clothes wires. 'How did this happen to me?' she thought as she disappeared back into her house.

In the awkwardness of his tumble into the fence, the blood rushing from Aleksandr's palm splattered across his face and he looked far worse than he actually was. Zita cried out, "Oh my God, my God, daddy, you're hurt, daddy. Daddy, daddy you're hurt."

Attempting to right himself, Aleksandr hadn't noticed his gash or the blood and just growled, "God damn him."

"You devil. You Satan. Aiiiieeeeahhh!" Zita shrieked, rushing my father who'd been standing dazed, the belt dangling by his side, images of his bicycle-beating crowding his awareness. The sight of her, like the rampage of light blazing from the nose of a smoke-belching locomotive, snapped my father to alert. He raised his hands to protect himself as Zita, her fingernails flared and pointed at his eyes, charged wildly and barreled into him knocking him to the ground.

"Eddie," my mother yelled, reflexively, not out of care for him but because she could not stand the gossip of her husband in a brawl with the next-door neighbor girl spreading through the people in the community. She knew it would and how would she face them? "Eddie, stop," she shouted, an absurd almost comic thought since it was my father who was on the ground.

"Bo, do something," Irene ordered. She did not feel the right to do something herself or she would have. No matter how well she may have been accepted into the Niemiec clan, this was Bo's territory and not her place.

Zita threw herself on my father, wailing and kicking and punching, a frenzied barrage of wrath and madness, sobbing and shrieking, landing several fierce blows before my father flung her aside just in time to see Ari jump the fence and knock Aleksandr, who was about to kick my father in the head, back against the fence. Ari stood in front of Aleksandr keeping him penned.

My father got to his feet but I had to shout, "Dad, watch out."

He turned to see Zita, who had scrambled to her feet, launch herself at him again. This time he wasn't careful. She had to be stopped, and stopped cold. Just as she reached him he grabbed her and flung her with such force that she stumbled backward until she bounced off the wall of the barn and slumped to the ground, her eyes bulging in surprise and pain.

"My God," Vi gasped, covering her breasts with her arms. Although the community of her childhood was by no means wealthy, factory workers and laborers for the most part, she'd never witnessed such violence, and particularly male-on-female ferocity. "Chez," she whimpered. Chez ran over and held her. "I got you, honey. It's okay. I got you."

"Take me home, Chez."

"I can't, honey." The Brothers had to back each other.

"I want to go home."

"Not right now. Why don't you go inside?"

"No. I want to stay with you."

"Okay, Vi. I'm here. I'm here."

Agnes moaned and uncurled, a large welt on her face.

My father, glaring, turned toward Aleksandr.

I'd never heard my father or anyone breathe the way my father was breathing: husky, harsh, and yet hollow, mostly through his mouth. The angle of the light from the post in the alley split his face in two, dark and light, invisible and visible. I couldn't read him. I had no idea what he was going to do.

"Stop him, Bo, stop Eddie," Irene ordered, but Bo paid her little mind. "Do you hear me, Bo?"

I began to run for the alley on my way to Aleksandr's yard when my mother grabbed me. "Stay here, Jimmy. Stay here." I resisted and tried to free myself but she wrapped her arms around me with a tight jerk. "I said stay here."

Ari, who was still keeping Aleksandr at bay near the fence shouted, "Hey, God damn it, Chez, I need help here." That one moment's distraction allowed Aleksandr the chance and, with one arm, he heaved Ari to the side and rushed my father like a boxer charging out of his corner of the ring.

"Kill the son-of-a-bitch," Julli bellowed, "kill 'im."

My father's adrenalin surged into full fight mode. He latched onto Aleksandr's hands, which were raised for the attack, and with his powerful will, physical strength, and without a sound, my father forced Aleksandr's arms down causing his head to fall forward in a bow of deference.

Aleksandr forced his head up and roared, "Aaaahhhhh," into father's face.

"Oooahhhhh," my father roared back pinning Aleksandr's hands to his sides and then roared again, "Aaaaahhhh."

"Kill the son-of-a-bitch," Julli whispered in a delirium of his own.

After a moment's paralytic standoff, Aleksandr hissed, "*Ty bękareiel*" (You bastard) and spit in my father's face.

"*Jestem bękartem? Ja? Bękartem?*" (I'm the bastard? Me? Bastard?) My father rocked Aleksandr a step to the right and threw him left toward the middle of the yard. Aleksandr, his arms flopping in an awkward spread-eagle, wobbled backward out of control, fell, and moaned reaching for his back.

Agnes had made a round flower garden in the center of the yard and defined it with a circle of bricks dug in at a forty-five-degree angle. Aleksandr landed hard on the edge of one of the bricks, jamming him just under his right shoulder blade. He moaned and lay still.

"Did ya kill'im, Ketchup?"

Bo, followed by Irene, dashed through the alley into the next yard.

Irene went to Aleksandr.

Bo carefully put his arm around my father, not knowing whether my father would swing at him or not.

"Easy, Eddie, easy," Bo whispered. He was the only one, besides my mother, who knew about the thrashing Louie had given my father when he smashed his bike. "You okay?"

My father, struggling with the fierce emotional swirl whipsawing his insides, didn't answer. From the day Louie demolished "The Eddie" my father had done his best to muzzle his thoughts and quell his feelings. It was in the dark of that night, as he lay awake in pain, sorrow and rage, fending off a feeling of collapse, that he vowed never, never, never to let anyone know what had happened and how he felt, and he would start with himself. He would forget it. So whenever his father's contorted face rose in his imagination he refused to be frightened by it, punching his thigh to distract himself. And when tears arose he would, with the fury of his will, force himself not to cry, not to show any sign of weakness or capitulation. And, for the most part, he succeeded.

But Aleksandr's belt broke through the bulwark my father had so carefully built against himself and released a brutal cascade of memories and feelings.

"What?" my father whispered.

"How you doin'?"

"I wanted to kill him, Bo. If he'd come at me again," his voice trailed off leaving behind a vacuum of uncertainty.

"It's okay, Eddie. It's okay."

"I might have killed him."

"But you didn't."

"I wanted to. I could've. If he'd come..."

"I know."

"It would've been easy."

"Yeah."

They looked at each other and into each other. A bond of deep understanding and silent masculine care passed between them. The roar of feelings passing through my father's body began to subside.

"I would've."

Agnes, wounded and in pain, crawled to the center of the yard and knelt beside her father. Seeing the blood on his face and shirt she gasped, "Papa. You're hurt, papa." She cradled his head in her lap and stroked it. "It's okay, Papa, I'm here, I'm here."

"My back," he whispered. "I hurt in my back."

"Where, Papa?"

"In my back."

Agnes reached around and found the injured spot. Aleksandr winced and cried out. "Don't push, you stupid girl."

"I'm sorry, Papa."

Zita rushed to the circle. "You stupid girl, Agnes." She pushed Agnes aside and yanked Aleksandr to her. He fell into her lap, his head between her bare legs which had been exposed when the bottom of her nightgown dropped open. "I'm here for you, Papa. I'm here."

"Aaahhh," he cried out again. "Get away you filthy girl. I can smell you." He flung Zita aside, reaching up to pull Agnes' head to his, whispering, "My daughter. My daughter."

"But me, Papa," Zita begged. "I'm covered now, Papa. I'm your daughter too."

Aleksandr closed his eyes and lay still.

Fearing the worst possible outcome, Irene touched his throat. "I can feel his pulse." Her sigh revealed her relief. "Let's get him in the house."

Ari and Bo helped stand Aleksandr up. Irene took Agnes by the arm and they all disappeared into the house.

My father passed through their back gate and into the alley.

My mother tightened her arms around me. I could feel she was crying.

Chez pulled Vi closer, her arms wrapped tightly across her breasts.

Julli let go the wires and fell to his knees. He whispered, "Did'ya kill 'im, Ketchup?"

Zita remained on her knees at the flower circle, weeping.

He's Not My People

It took a while before the family could gather back together. The shock at Aleksandr's rampage bred a quiet that stilled even the walls and floors of our old wood frame house. Under everyday conditions the house resounded with creaks and squeaks and groans. But it seemed the house itself retreated, terrified into silence.

Chez led Vi into the basement: perhaps from a need for familiarity; or perhaps from blind habit; or perhaps it was as far away as he thought he could get from the madness.

Watching Vi, who stood near the furnace with her back to him, he arranged two chairs at the pinochle table and placed them so that he and Vi would be knee-to-knee. But when he called her over she chose a chair on the opposite side of the table and wouldn't look at him.

"What's goin' on Vi?"

Looking down at the table she clasped her hands as though she might be praying. "I wanted to leave, Chez. Why didn't we leave when I asked?"

Trapped between his love for Vi and his allegiance to The Brothers, Chez said simply, "I couldn't."

Vi brought her gaze up to meet his. "Why not?"

"Just in case somebody needed me," he answered simply as though the rightness of his reason was self-evident.

Chez and Vi had been together for nine years, married seven, and yet she stared at him as though she'd never met him. "They didn't need you, Chez. Didn't you see that?"

He cocked his head to one side like a puppy in wonder. "They didn't?"

"Ari yelled for me."

"But you didn't go, Chez."

He blinked and shifted in his chair. "Just in case, Vi. It was just in case."

"But what about me, Chez? I needed you." Her blue eyes filmed over and her tears fell.

As though remembering a crime he'd committed, forgotten, and was suddenly faced with its truth, he couldn't speak. He felt like a boy, a boy who'd committed a grievous sin.

Words spun circles in his head, smashing into one another. If those colliding fragments had lined up in lucid logical order presenting him with the most convincing rationale, he still wouldn't have known what to say because he hadn't listened to his beloved Vi. He hadn't listened. And for penance it wasn't a matter of saying ten Our Fathers and ten Hail Marys. He was already suffering the scourge of his own guilt for not having chosen her.

Then everything stopped and he heard himself whisper, "Jees, Vi, I'm sorry."

"I needed you, Chez."

He reached out for her hand. She pulled away.

As she walked to the other side of the furnace where she couldn't be seen he heard her moan, "I needed you."

After Ari had helped Aleksandr into his house, he returned looking for Blanche. He found her on our back-porch steps curled into herself. "You okay, Blanche?" She was dazed and scared.

"Is this what your people are like?" she whispered.

"My people? What do you mean 'my people'?"

"He beat her..."

"He's not my people—"

"He wanted to hurt her—"

"Blanka..."

"He wanted to."

"My people don't do that."

She looked away, shaking her head, trying to understand what was completely beyond her reach.

"How can you say my people, Blanche? You know me. I'm not like that."

"He wanted to."

Ari and Blanche had had their spats, especially regarding her mother's interference in their marriage, and yet they always came back together, often ending up in bed. But he'd never before seen her so withdrawn. He couldn't feel her. He was sitting right next to her with his arm around her waist and he couldn't feel her. She was right there and not there and that scared him.

"Let's go in, Blanche."

She rose, mechanically, dutifully, and followed him through the kitchen.

"Ari..." my mother started.

"Not now, Helch. Not now."

They continued on into my bedroom. They sat on the bed.

"Blanche, look at me." She did but barely, "I'm not like him, Blanche. He's not my people. He's not."

In the front room, Janice had squeezed herself into the very corner of the couch clinging to the picture album her mother had brought for her. Seeing her I realized she hadn't come out to the back yard.

"Where were you?" I asked, hesitant to sit next to her.

"Where?" she whispered so low I could hardly hear her. She barely moved. I'd never seen her so timid.

Suddenly she was very small, like a tiny sparrow. She looked so fragile, delicate and imaginary. I felt sorry for her. I wanted to protect her, to comfort her. Then she slammed back to normal size, quickly, abruptly. I actually stepped back, intimidated. But I couldn't release the kindliness I'd felt.

"In the backyard," I said, gently, and decided to sit next to her.

"Leave me alone," she snapped, turning away as much as the couch corner would permit.

"What did I do?" I blurted.

"I said leave me alone."

"What did I...?"

I'd done it again, approached her only to be rebuffed. Again. A powerful anger rushed through me.

I'd had it with her. Her you're-a-crud attitude overwhelmed any feelings of attraction and care I'd felt for her.

"You're mean," I attacked. "You know that?"

She moved the album from her lap to her chest.

"And you're crazy."

"I am not crazy."

"Yes, you are. You're mean and crazy."

"I saw in the yard."

"What did you see? You weren't even in the yard."

"I saw. I saw."

"Why didn't you come out?"

Janice turned her face away and slumped into herself. "Leave me alone."

As I stared at her, images of the belt slashing across Agnes' back flashed in my imagination followed by cries, blood, pleas, and Aleksandr's eyes. I didn't want them but couldn't control them.

Just then I heard Bo and Irene coming in from Aleksandr's house. Their voices released me from Janice and from the couch. I ran into the kitchen. The room was filled with the acrid stench of eucalyptus, camphor, and menthol.

"What stinks?" I gagged, struggling to regain myself.

"Agnes gave Bo a jar of Vick's Vapo-Rub," Irene told my mother. "He rubbed it into Aleksandr's back. The old man's got a nasty bruise. Christ, it's black. The size of an orange, maybe a grapefruit. And ya know what? When the old man moaned, Agnes grabbed my hand. She squeezed it hard. Really hard. Then we just watched."

"How is he?" my mother asked.

"I'm not a doctor. How the hell would I know? Okay, I guess."

Contempt swelled across her face like a second skin.

Bo reached under the sink for the detergent, washed his hands, opened a Strohs, went to the dining room table, and sat alone.

"How's Agnes?" my mother asked.

"She didn't talk a lot...more worried about her father. After what he did? Can you believe it? She's worried about him. After what he did." Irene filled a shot glass with Seven Crown. "What the hell happened? What'd she do?"

"I don't know." My mother's hands trembled and her body buzzed with fear, so she sat down at the table. "I never saw her wearing pants before...maybe...I don't know."

"He beat her for pants?"

"I don't know... maybe..."

"That's crazy."

"That man is crazy," my mother said. "Always has been. Crazy with religion. But I had no idea he could..."

Irene stared down into her Seven Crown. "The son-of-a-bitch."

Both women withdrew into their own internal refuge for a moment's peace and control. But this time what had before been a reliable source of protection and comfort for my mother erupted into a nonstop spasm of lashes, blood, and screams. My mother stood abruptly and braced herself against the table. Irene, trembling, left my mother alone in the kitchen and sat as close to Bo as he would allow.

My mother stayed in the kitchen and began arranging the food on the table as though she expected everyone to return, fill a plate, and go back to playing cards. She'd put on an apron, which she hadn't been wearing before Aleksandr's outrage. As she arranged the table, hardly touching anything, she wiped her hands on the apron for no reason that I could see, wrinkling it.

I'd never felt anything like I felt that night. A deadness penetrated the house, more like a clotted-over fear. Maybe because my father hadn't returned yet and there was no one in the house strong enough to keep us safe.

CRASH. The outside door to the back yard flung open with such force that one of the hinges bent preventing the door from closing correctly.

"Where the fuck is everybody?" Holding himself up in the damaged doorway, Julli sent a twisted blast of rage through the house. "You all deaf?"

Not getting a quick enough response, he started up the stairs toward the kitchen. Fogged with too much Strohs and Seven Crown, he couldn't see clearly. His distorted perspective caused his foot to catch the edge of the second step, sending him crashing hard onto his knees. "Son-of-a-bitch," he wailed falling back onto the landing, his head just missing the *beczka.* "These fuckin' stairs. I told you Ketchup they weren't built right. Nobody fucking listens to me."

"Julli, hang on," Chez urged coming up from the basement.

"Julli, stay where you are," my mother cautioned, heading down from the kitchen.

I stood at the top of the stairs startled by the pleasure I felt watching Julli flop around on the landing, and yet wary that he might get his balance and come in my direction.

"Don't fucking tell me what to do. I'm tired of people telling me what to do." Julli managed to get himself onto his wobbly hands and knees which allowed my mother, who sat on the bottom step, to reach out and bring him toward her, cradling him in her lap.

"*Shh, shh, shh,* Julli, *sshhhh,*" my mother whispered, 'I'm here now."

"For fuck's sake, Helen, leave me alone," he hollered but did not pull himself away from her. "Leave me the fuck alone."

Chez, swamped in the undertow of guilt and remorse for how he'd treated Vi snarled, "Shut the hell up, Julli. That's your sister. You need her right now."

"Need? I don't need no fuckin' body. I don't need her and I sure as hell don't need you."

Chez grabbed Julli by the shirt and shook him hard. "Stop being such an asshole."

Taller, stronger, and meaner, if Julli, had been sober, he could've torn Chez to pieces. Instead Julli plunged into a wretched and pitiful self-disgust.

"I'm sorry, Helcha. I am such a shit."

"It's okay, Julli, it's okay." My mother drew his head to her chest. "You're not a bad boy, Julli."

"I am. I am. I've always been. I can't help it. There's something wrong with me," Julli pleaded.

"Cut that shit out, Julli." Chez's eyes filled with tears. Not for Julli. For himself and Vi. "There's nothing wrong with you."

"The fuck there isn't," Julli choked. "What the fuck do you know?"

Of course, everyone knew there was something wrong with Julli, but, aside from his drinking, no one could say what. Given the education level of the neighborhood, and the teaching at Queen of Angels that only faith in God could lead us out of misery, and the Old-Country suspicion of anything that wasn't already known, and the family's determination to keep blind to what they suspected but were too frightened to face, there was little possibility that the ache that haunted Julli would ever be recognized let alone understood. His protest was justified. They knew nothing.

"Aarrrh," he cried out, a cry as much pathetic as menacing, his arms thrashing as he tried to free himself from my mother and Chez. "Where am I?"

"Julli, Julli," my mother rocked him, holding his head between her breasts. "You're here, Julli, with me. You're here." I'd never seen her behave that way before, not with me, nor my father, nor with any of The Brothers.

"Here? Where the fuck is here?"

Ari arrived just as Julli lashed out with his fist in my mother's direction, inadvertently, perhaps willfully, striking her on the shoulder. "Chez," Ari ordered, "we have to pin him down." Ari pulled Julli's head away from my mother's chest.

"No Ari, no," she resisted.

"God damn it, Helen, don't be stupid. He's drunk and dangerous." Ari grabbed the wrist of Julli's loose arm and he and Chez pulled Julli away, standing him on his knees on the landing. "Get upstairs Helen. Now."

My mother frantically scrambled away, finding herself in the arms of Irene who was standing in the doorway. Realizing that Irene had witnessed her babying Julli, my mother pulled away to the other side of the porch. I tried to get out of her way but she crashed into me and then turned her face to the windows.

"Rrrrraaa," Julli growled as he twisted and squirmed resisting their grip.

Ari shook Julli hard. "Listen to me, brother. You're drunk. Stupid drunk. Stop fighting and we'll take you in. If you don't we'll throw your ass in the yard. What's it gonna be?"

Julli stiffened and he puffed out his chest.

"Don't fuckin' try it, Julli, or we'll tear your ass apart," Ari snarled.

They stared, nose to nose, until Julli, his strength collapsed, sunk into a weak and weepy self-pity.

"I'm sorry, Ari. I'm sooo sorry." He looked at Ari as best as the Seven Crown and Strohs would permit. Then he pushed his mouth toward Ari's face.

Ari pulled back. "What're you doing?"

"You're my brother, my good brother, and I love you."

"I love you too, Julli."

"I want a kiss." He pursed his limp lips but his mouth dropped open.

"God damn it, Julli you're fucking drunk," Ari held him at arm's length.

Julli closed his mouth and pursed again, and again his mouth dropped open. "I'm drunk. Okay. But I still want a kiss." He tried moving toward Ari.

Ari grabbed him hard by the ears. "You got your head up your ass."

Julli laughed. "Not a bad place for it sometimes, right?"

"God damn you, Julli, you can be such a dick."

Julli wailed as though stabbed. "I can't help it, brother. I can't. You must hate me for being an asshole."

"Just stop."

"Okay, Ari. Okay." Julli's body went limp. "I'll stop."

"Chez, let's get him inside."

They put his arms over their shoulders and stood him up.

"Just a little kiss, Ari." A sharp pain shot through Julli's knees and they buckled.

"For Christ's sake, Julli, help us," Chez barked.

"Christ, Jesus Christ, our lord and savior," Julli giggled. "Can't have your head up your ass and get saved."

"Stand up straight." Chez put his fist into Julli's lower back forcing Julli erect. "Lock your knees."

Julli locked his knees. "Like a soldier, hey Chez, like you in the Army."

"Yeah, brother, like in the Army."

They started up the stairs. "Jesus you're heavy." Chez adjusted Julli's weight against his own.

At the kitchen door, my mother pointed to the chair at the table. "Put him there." As they maneuvered Julli into the chair he recoiled.

"Jesus Christ what stinks? It's God damn Vick's. I don't need no God damn Vick's." He stood and Ari and Chez reached out for him. "Leave me alone. I'm not a baby. Ask

Helen. I'm a man. Right, Helen. I'm a big boy. You remember. Right?"

"Julli, you need to sit," my mother screamed with surprising force.

Julli turned to her and grinned. "You remember, right?"

"God damn it, Julli," Chez punched him hard on the arm, "sit the fuck down."

"No," Julli roared. "I don't need to sit." He spotted the Seven Crown on the sink bar. "I need a shot. That's what I need. Come on, boys, a shot and a beer. How 'bout it?" He started toward the sink.

Ari made a move to stop him. Julli shoved him hard, sending him across the kitchen bouncing off the stove. "Stay the fuck away. When a man needs a drink, he needs a drink."

At that moment, my father appeared at the kitchen door. "Julli, stop," he ordered. The sound of my father's voice stopped Julli cold.

At first Julli didn't turn and everyone in the house, including me, wondered what he would do. My father had challenged him before but it was always about something, his work, his ideas, his drinking. This time it was about Julli himself, his person, his manhood. He'd been given a direct order. What would he do?

When he did turn to face my father, he turned slowly, deliberately, ominously, his eyes half shut and clouded, his jaw tight and jutted, though his arms were at his sides his fists were clenched. All the years of rivalry between them pulsed in the room.

Finally, Julli whispered, "Ketchup, did you kill the son-of-a-bitch?"

"No."

"You could've."

"I know."

"You should've. I wished you would've."

Another shot of pain pierced Julli's knee. As he reached for it he saw large wet spots at his knees. "My pants are wet."

"I watered the lawn today. The grass is wet," my father said calmly.

"Fuck," Julli smiled. "I wet my pants. You see that Ketchup," Julli laughed full out. "I wet my pants."

"Julli," my father said with care, almost affection, "It's time to go home."

A dark veil fell across Julli's face. He seemed to be thinking it over. After a long pause he said, "Yeah, Ketchup. It's time, time to go home."

I actually heard a collective sigh in the room.

"I wished you'd'a killed him, Ketchup. Lousy bastard."

"It's time," my father said.

"Yeah," Julli mumbled. "You know what, Ketchup?"

"What?"

"I gotta take a leak."

"The toilet's right behind you, Julli," my mother gestured to the bathroom.

"Helen, how many years I lived in this house? How many times I pissed in that toilet? You don't think I know where it is?"

"You know where it is, Julli. You know."

"But Eddie says it's time I go home. I'll piss in my own toilet. Okay?"

"Okay Julli. Okay."

"It's over now," my father commanded gently. "Time for everybody to go."

"*Do domu* (To home)," Julli announced, one forefinger raised slightly above his head like a captain in charge of launching an expedition. "*Do domu.*"

Julli shuffled toward the back door with his hands over his crotch. "I hope I get home," he squealed in a high-pitched child's voice, "don't want to pee my pants again," laughing aloud, "what would I tell momma?"

Vi, who'd come up from the basement, stood in the doorway. Julli bowed to her, a flamboyant formal bow sweeping his arm past her with a flourish. "Allow me to let you pass, my dazzling beauty." The danger in his voice was palpable, forcing Vi, who loathed the thought of being touched by him, to press herself against the door jamb. When she saw enough room she quickly squeezed past but was unable to escape Julli swatting her on the rump. She screamed and ran past Chez into the front room, less from the violence Julli was capable of, and more from not wanting to be dirtied by his ugly, adolescent sexuality.

"Thought you'd get away, eh, my pretty? But I got ya now didn't I, got me a hand full."

"You're such an asshole, Julli," Chez sighed and followed Vi into the front room.

"Whole ass," Julli taunted, "whole ass," raising his triumphant handful to the ceiling, "got a piece of the whole ass, Chezy boy."

"Julli," my father warned.

"Oops, just playin', Eddie, just playin'."

"It's time, Julli."

"I'm goin' Eddie, I'm goin.' I'll piss in my own toilet." He stepped into the darkness of the back porch.

Menace, stuffed away in the underbelly of our family's daily life—exposed in anxious gestures and furtive glances, in the tiny yet persistent humiliations called teasing, in overt backbiting and crushing contempt, the habituated lack of regard evoking the routine denial, "I was just kidding. What are you being so sensitive for?"—surfaced that night, up from a deep and primitive lair, piercing through the family psyche, opening a sharp and bewildering confusion that left everyone rummaging around, searching not for a coat or a purse, but internally, for what to do or how to be. They desperately wanted to restore what had been there just an hour before. Not the pinochle and beer, but the familiarity, the expected and rehearsed scenes, their authorized and approved roles, their practiced and polished lines, in short, the enveloping life of the family. They didn't know where to find it and had no idea where to look.

They had been gut-punched by Aleksandr's unbridled cruelty and pathetic impotence, horrifying yet unsettlingly recognizable. What the family had grown accustomed to, the beliefs and behaviors upon which they'd built their new world, their sense of identity, propriety, and custom, what everyone had come to accept as just-the-way-things-are, receded into the walls and floors.

Something new had slithered to life between them and around them and within them, a realization they couldn't deny—that Aleksandr's violence, though extreme, was no different in kind than what the family kept housed in smiles and silence, Strohs and Seven Crown, in the secrets they told about each other, and the slights they endured. They hadn't conjured this awareness. It arose unbidden. And they couldn't keep it at bay.

Bo, still in his chair at the dining room table, nervously spun his Strohs bottle round and around, until he threw back a mouthful and whispered to himself but loud enough that everyone heard, "What are we?"

The close of a typical pinochle and poker evening would be filled with "Thanks," and "See you next week," and "Let's have one for the road." But uncertainty hung in the house like a thick fog reducing to near zero everyone's ability to think much less move forward.

My mother unconsciously wrung her hands in her apron, drawing it up toward her waist, compressing it into a crumpled ball so tightly it could no longer be contained between her fingers. Suddenly the apron burst forth as though it had come alive and bit her to gain its release.

"Owww," she yelped, drawing everyone's attention. Realizing what she'd done, shame flooded her body, her face becoming fiery red, the heat in her skin making public what should have remained private. She wasn't naked. She was worse than naked. She was foolish, ashamed, exposed, and open to view.

"Before you go," she fluttered, grabbing her apron as though she was properly and appropriately cleaning her hands, "take home some of the food. There's so much left."

Taking food home at the end of the evening was customary. According to the ritual, the host always provided more food than could be eaten so there would be food to take way.

"Baloney, rye bread, head cheese, kielbasa, and Vernors. I have some Vernors I was saving for tomorrow. Anna's got gas and she likes a little Vernors in the morning. But that's okay. I'll get more. Take, take."

"Not tonight," my father whispered.

"But we always take..." not having enough breath to finish. She looked to Bo and Irene. My father turned away.

Ari came to her from my bedroom and took her hand. "Not tonight, Helen." He put his arm around her waist. "It's okay. Next time."

"But..."

"*Shh, shh, shh*, Helch. Next time. Okay?"

"Okay, Ari." Hers was the voice of a child.

Bo stood up silently, which everyone understood as the signal to leave.

The house stirred, coming back to life; slowly, cautiously. A chair moved. The floor squeaked, faintly. Ari retrieved Blanche from my bed. Janice placed a rubber band around the picture album she clutched to her chest. Vi, leaning against the wall near the front door, her arms wrapped across her breasts, glanced to Chez who promptly moved closer to her side.

I'd remained in the kitchen away from the group, which was my wont, feeling deeply part of my family and yet not a part of it at all. I couldn't have said it then but I knew the displacement they all felt: a displacement even family blood and bonds could not overcome; a distance reaching back to the fields of Poland, where people in the villages, notwithstanding their customs, language, and history, felt separate from one another, disconnected and alone. But no matter. Life had to be lived. Whatever the circumstances, life had to be lived. My family had to live, to go forward.

I felt my heart beat, dully. I watched my family struggle with choices they'd made many, many times before—cheek kisses, hugs, a parting joke, announcements for the upcoming week. But now, in the shock and disruption, they were befuddled. Their simple, ritualized departure demanded more of them than they were capable of.

I too felt adrift. The moorings which were supposed to provide stability and a sense of trust, a safe and secure hold, had come loose and I was on my own.

I closed my eyes and a sound emanated from within the darkness; a gurgling sound, thick, raspy, like a croak underwater. I opened my eyes expecting the sound to vanish with the light, but I heard it again, from behind me. And then again, deeper, insistent.

I stepped onto the back porch and heard the sound coming from outside. I stepped down toward the outside door and saw it was partially open. I could see one of the hinges was bent preventing the door from closing. As I reached for the handle thinking I would close it, I heard the sound again, loud, from my right. I turned toward it and began screaming, "Dad. Daddy. Daddy. Daaaadddd."

My father came running with Bo behind him.

Lit by the light from the lamppost in the alley, Uncle Julli was hanging on that stretch of the chain link fence where he had bent the wires upward to keep the sparrows away, the pointed tips speared into his throat.

Uncle Bo grabbed me as my mother, Irene, Ari, and Chez came out into the yard.

"Stay away," my father commanded.

Uncle Julli gurgled once more, blood spurting from his throat onto the cement patio he cared for with such pride. He seized upward, his back stiffening. It looked like he might free himself from the spikes, but he collapsed down and the points pushed even further into his throat.

His body limp, knees on the ground, his shirt and pants soaked in the blood dripping onto his patio, his fingers wrapped around the crossbar at the top, he was still.

"Is he...?" my mother gasped.

"Stay away," my father ordered again.

I wanted to move toward the fence to see better but Uncle Bo held me back. My mother moaned and collapsed. Irene was able to catch her fall and gently laid her on the ground. Ari and Chez stared.

Uncle Julli was dead.

God Damn It, Julli

Tradition in our community, which echoed the practice of my grandparents' old-country villages, called for the body of the dead to be placed-in-state in the house of the deceased's birth. In respect of that tradition all of the furniture in our living room had been removed to other parts of the house to make space for Julli's casket.

His body lay in our front room surrounded by funereal wreaths, their fragrances suffusing the house with an almost viscous sweetness that turned into a sickly, inescapable stench.

When my grandfather Antoni passed his body remained in our living room for three days and three nights, allowing those who had to travel a distance to make the trip and pay their respects, and for most of that time my father stayed awake in a chair near the coffin making certain nothing disturbed the body, a precaution, even at age seven, I thought was bizarre—after all, who would want to disturb it and why? And so it was with Julli, tucked away in his coffin in our front room for an equal number of days and nights.

During the vigil for Antoni I was too young to notice the job the undertaker had performed to make him look as good as possible. Cancer killed Antoni in his sleep. There wasn't much to see so I wasn't interested. But when Julli's body first arrived in his coffin, and I had a moment alone with him, I approached the casket wanting to see the gash marks on his throat. But his shirt collar had been buttoned and a tie served as a lock to keep his collar, raised high along his neck, from revealing the gashes—except for one small pink and serrated section, about a quarter of an inch long, at the side of his neck farthest from me.

I looked around to make certain I wouldn't be seen because I'd decided I would touch the jagged spot. I even considered pulling the collar down so the marks would show. With courage and some creepiness that hyper-tunneled my attention I watched my arm extend and my forefinger point, ready to explore what I knew was forbidden to touch. My finger floated past his nearest shoulder, over his face where I could make out the hairs in his nose, over the curve of his chin, falling toward the red wound, hesitating, deciding whether or not I should go through with it, then committing to push through the butterflies rioting in my belly, until—

"What are you doing?" my mother barked in alarm, shattering my intention.

I whipped back my arm and spun to look at her. She had Anna's forbidding face, brows furrowed, lips drawn inward and tight, arms crossed over her chest, eyes squinted focusing her accusing gaze.

"Nothing," I defended myself, weakly.

"What were you doing?" she insisted. She seemed as tall as the ceiling and looked more like a man than my mother.

My mouth dried up. Bile rose into my throat and I could taste it. Electric fear tingled through me. I knew I had to say something. I ran my tongue across my lips, softening them with as much moisture as I could draw from the corners of my mouth. "I heard a dead person's body is cold," I explained, the words sucking away whatever saliva remained. "I wanted to touch Uncle Julli's face to see."

"You're lying." Her giant head pushed up against the ceiling.

I wanted to confess, hoping that honesty would generate spittle to swab my mouth, but her face told me the risk was too great. She looked like Anna. "I'm not."

A long moment passed before she uncrossed her arms, opened her eyes a bit, and slowly shrunk back down to size. "Get away from there. And I don't want to see you touching Julli. Ever."

"Okay." I stood still until I saw her face relax a bit more. "I won't." I took a small, tentative, arbitrary step not knowing how to leave the room.

"Get away from him." Words shot out of her mouth like bullets, snapping me out of my confoundment.

"Okay. Okay." I bolted through the front door and onto the porch. When I heard the door slam behind me I flushed with the relief of being free, and I realized, for the first time, just how alike my mother and Anna were: not merely how they looked but who they were. My mother truly was her mother's daughter with the addition of an understandable deep-seated fear, the consequence of having been Anna's child.

My heart rushed with compassion. I knew how I felt around Anna, but she wasn't my mother. Even though the nuns at Queen of Angels would say that she was my grandmother and that obedience to her was the will of God and anything else was sinful, jeopardizing my sacred soul, I knew I didn't have to obey her. But my mother did.

A picture of my mother as a little girl cowering, Anna standing over her like a forbidding giant, seized my imagination, and I felt an intense sympathy for my mother, a sympathy I'd never known for anyone before.

I looked back through the front window and saw my mother standing over the coffin. She had Julli's collar between her fingers and raised it to fully cover the wounds, especially that little tag end that had been exposed. She bent and kissed him on the forehead, wiped away tears, stood for a moment more, then headed toward the kitchen.

Slowly, I walked between the houses, overtaken by my first experience of what I knew then to call love. Even though it came upon me unannounced and unbidden I knew it was deliberate, conscious love. And it hurt.

In the backyard Julli had incorrectly mixed the elements for his concrete patio leaving it more porous than it otherwise would have been so the stains from his blood were still visible no matter how many times and how hard Van had scrubbed it. His death had released her from the imprisonment of a marriage that would not permit divorce, and the rigor and fierce intention she applied to removing the stains gave evidence of her desire to be free of him. Some of the old women gossiped about her feral scrubbing. They believed she should be in mourning. But Van continued to scrub, removing more of Julli's remnant from the cement and from her soul with every scour.

The night Julli died my father took charge and I got to see his inherent power and authority. The strength of his presence as a man, as a human, radiated inspiration and, without quarrel, everyone acknowledged his leadership.

He behaved as a man born to face crisis; sure, deliberate, calm, clear, and caring. Before anyone could do anything, he kept them away from Julli's body. He knew the scene should not be disturbed and instructed Ari to call the police.

Irene raised my mother onto wobbly legs and shepherded her into the house. Vi and Blanche, who'd been watching from the back porch, followed along. Irene had once been forced, until help arrived, to take care of a man in the factory who accidentally had two fingers cut off when his hand slipped into the machine he worked on and he vomited, falling to the floor. It was under her leadership that the three women gave their attention to my mother who'd been overwhelmed by shock. Her lips pale and her face sunken they sat her down at the kitchen table reassuring her that everything would be all right.

As Ari called the police Irene told him to ask for an ambulance, adding, "We're gonna need a priest."

With a riot of sirens, the police and ambulance arrived, arousing the entire block, bringing people from both ends toward our house. Some of the policemen set up lines to prevent anyone from coming into the back yard while others examined Julli's body assuring themselves that he was dead, and then set about determining what had happened.

As the ambulance crew removed his body from the fence the police noticed the front of his pants were soaked. He smelled of urine and the zipper on his pants was opened with his penis hanging out. After they questioned everybody, including me—I was a little scared but mostly excited that they wanted to talk with me because I was the first to find him—they learned that his last words were, "I'll piss in my own toilet."

They concluded that Julli, very drunk, very unstable, must have had an urgent need to relieve himself and decided to urinate into the flower bed on our side of the fence. They imagined him leaning forward, supporting himself with one hand against the top bar of the fence, holding his penis in the other. He must have lost his balance and fell onto the wire tips which penetrated his throat, a conclusion no one disputed. According to the slash marks on his throat, he had struggled to free himself but didn't have the clear-headedness or coordination to pull himself away and so he bled to death.

I stayed in the yard watching the police work until I looked up and saw Anna silhouetted in the second-floor window, motionless, hovering over the scene. She scared me more than Julli's dying and I ran inside to my bedroom and shut the door. Anna didn't come down for the rest of that evening.

After Julli's death a scandal erupted in the neighborhood. Some people denounced him as a "drunken mucker and no damn good."

"How could he be pissing in his mother's yard?"
"His pecker was hanging out, for Christ's sake."
"He was always a dumb ox."
"I kept my little girls in the house when he was out."
"He brought shame on everybody. *Wstyd. Wstyd.*"
"He shouldn't be buried in sacred ground."

My family was aware of what was going on around them, especially my mother, but shock coupled with the details of police reports and planning for Julli's burial kept them largely immune. The police suggested an autopsy just to be certain nothing unusual occurred in the way Julli died, but my mother, following my father's lead, declined. How much more humiliation could they bear? An official city ambulance showing up in front of the house, the word "coroner" emblazoned on its side, Julli's corpse loaded into the back and taken away to the county morgue, then delivered to the funeral parlor, placed in a casket which would be delivered to the house creating another disruption, soaking the already hypercharged gossip with suspicions of satanic forces, because, to the plodding and paranoid peasant mind, the way Julli hung on the fence, his arms spread wide across the top bar, resembled Christ's pose on the cross, making a mockery of the Holy Crucifixion. Only Satan would be so depraved.

Besides, what could the coroner find that would make Julli's death any more unusual than it already was?

Those who inflamed the scandal had been insulted or injured by Julli. To them he was an irredeemable bully, a waste whose death could not have come sooner, and their retaliation spread beyond Julli's history to blister the family for "not raising him right" and not being able to control or sufficiently punish him.

In spite of Julli's reputation as wild and raging, much of which was justified, another faction emerged giving voice to compassion for him and care for the family. At first they appeared sharing cautious whispers asking, "How do you feel about Julli?"—a sincere question of interest and concern, feeling each other out so as not to give away their intent until they determined they were of the same heart. Julli was dead and that was good. "But how sad, and for the family." More love for Julli was felt and expressed than he ever knew during his life. People didn't understand him anymore than before, but they knew, deeply knew, that this life held no promise for him. He tried to escape on the rails, but couldn't. He tried to find redemption inside a bottle of Stroh's, but the more he drank the deeper the bottle became. Even his rage turned against him. It was best for Julli and for everyone that he was gone.

Charity balanced the scorn. Resentment was moderated by tenderness. A sense of deliverance, both for Julli and the family, quietly arose in our house. He was a good man in his heart, but his heart was broken. Best he should be in a better place. Although gruesome, through his death Julli finally found his way out.

Throughout the three days devoted to Julli's vigil family and friends arrived during appointed visitation hours to view the body and pay their last respects. The casket, surrounded by four church-sized candle arrangements sat at the center of the lifeless tableau which was held together by memorial ribbons draped between the candle stands, some swathed across wreaths, and others on the wall above the casket on either side of an image of the crucified Christ. "Beloved Son" and "Beloved Brother" had been printed across their sateen surfaces. "Beloved Husband" was noticeably absent.

All the chairs in the house including the metal folding chairs, our four as well as six more loaned by the church, were set up in the front room allowing people to sit vigil in Julli's presence, some silently and others chatting in whispers. Still others mingled throughout the house expressing their sympathy, visiting with each other, and eating the food my mother and Irene had prepared along with the casseroles and pastry some mourners provided, an offering of condolence and support that, for my mother was difficult to receive.

Candle smoke rose to the ceiling and curled into itself hovering like a twisting canopy over the casket, smoky formations resembling the clouds of heaven I'd seen on our church windows. At first I imagined Uncle Julli's soul in Heaven. Then I decided not enough time had passed since his death for his soul to have been purified and that definitely placed him in the mid-world of Purgatory. Even though I had hated him many times, now that he was dead, and in such an eerie way, I couldn't invoke, let alone justify, the thought that he might be in Hell.

Before the first day of the wake the funeral director delivered Julli to the house in his casket. As the funeral director set up the tripods for the wreaths, placed the golden candle stands, and draped the ribbons Anna broke her isolation and came downstairs without making a sound.

"Ma, what are you doing here?"

"I live here," Anna spit. Her thin pale skin, sagging and pleated by wear and resignation, eyes ringed in darkness where her death had already taken up residence biding its time, wispy disheveled hair from which color had fled years before, and a black babushka tied beneath her chin made her look like a soul condemned to wander the underworld without ever knowing why.

"I know that Ma, but why did you come down?"

"I need permission?"

Embarrassed in front of the director my mother tried to stop Anna. "Jesus, Ma…"

"Don't use Jesus' name," Anna sliced in.

"Maaaa, for God's sake…"

"*Wstyd.*"

"Okay, Ma, okay. What do you want?"

"*Chcę zobaczyć mojego syna*" (I want to see my son). As Anna turned toward the casket her words stopped my mother cold.

Anna had emotionally disavowed Julli when, twenty years earlier, and in spite of her bitter protests, he spoke of leaving to hobo around the country. In a jagged, guttural Polish she screamed, "You abandon the family, you abandon me, you abandon God. You are Judas and you will die, you will die on a tree by your neck."

Terrified, he begged to be forgiven. He promised never to leave, to stay and take care of her, to be with her, but she wouldn't hear it.

"Judas," she screamed. "Judas."

He desperately tried to win her back. "Momma, I was wrong. Momma, I love you. Momma." But she remained adamant.

"You care only for you. I can't trust you. No more."

Finally exhausted, Julli, in a rage, flew out of the house and caught a train along the tracks near our house and was gone.

So it was a true surprise when she said, "I want to see my son."

Anna stood over the casket, motionless, gripped by memories she could not forget: pictures of the past that stretched back before the New World, a world her father had told her she deserved because she was her family's hope for the future, a future that bore the seeds of corruption, a delusion that forced her to leave behind her imaginings of a pure and holy life in the church and the beautiful man she loved. When she looked down at Julli, who, of all her sons, was the most beautiful, the most like the man of her reveries, she raised her arms, slowly at first, and then more and more until they extended out to her sides, like rigid, catatonic wings able only to jerk and quiver, sending shudders to her torso which began to tremble.

"Ma, what's happening?" My mother grabbed Anna by the shoulders. "Ma, what're you doing?"

"I want to see my son."

"Ma, that's enough. Come on."

"I want to be with my son."

"Okay, Ma, okay. I'll bring you back later."

Anna screamed out, "Leave me alone you...you..." struggling for the words until she found just the one that would best express her contempt, "you girl. I want my son."

My mother spun Anna around and clutched her arms, lowering them, standing face to face. "Why now, Ma? Why? After all these years, now you want him? Now? Why?"

A darkness from the deepest pit of Anna's desecrated love and damnable capitulation rose and she hissed, "Because he was my favorite."

Anna had never revealed her feelings about Julli to anyone, although my mother had suspected, because throughout his life, before he left to ride the rails, Anna had indulged Julli in many ways and certainly more than his brothers or my mother.

"Come on, Ma."

Anna's meanness dissipated and she became confused, like a child looking for understanding and guidance.

"It's okay Ma. Come on, let's go upstairs. Come on."

Anna let herself be led up to the second floor. She never came down again during the wake nor did she attend Julli's funeral Mass. My mother asked if she wanted to go but she said, "No. I'll pray here," showing my mother the rosary she'd wrapped around her hands. "I'll pray to my blessed Mother Mary."

Father Paul, our pastor at Queen of Angels, a man of forty who wore thick glasses framed in black, with a thick mass of black curly hair, and who pulsed with vigor and energy, arrived at seven o'clock on the second night. It had been announced in church on Sunday that he would offer the wake ritual in Julli's behalf which caused there to be more people in the house than chairs, so the mourners extended through the dining room into the kitchen. Praying the rosary was the feature of the evening so most of the guests already had a rosary in their hands. Many were traditional beaded commercial rosaries, but some, held by the older people, were lengths of cord tied into the appropriate number of knots with a cord

Crucifix at the end. People had begun praying before Father Paul arrived.

My mother and The Brothers sat in the first row of chairs with one chair open for Father Paul to sit when he completed the prayer service. The Brothers' wives sat in the second row. My father and I sat together to one side of the room. I felt badly for him, because it didn't take much to notice how his place in my mother's family was only at the edge.

Upon his arrival, and after greeting everyone, Father Paul unfurled a midnight blue stole, adorned with yellow fringe and crosses embroidered at each end. He wore the garment to indicate he would be engaged in official priestly duties. Paul kissed both crosses and placed the stole around his neck, then knelt on the kneeler at the casket to pray privately and silently.

The parish loved him because he was a practical man, not overburdened with the demands of dogma. People felt close to him because he made himself available to them without judgment. They saw him as a priest to be revered because he was holy, and as a man who lived a real life among them, sharing their sorrows, celebrating their triumphs, dancing at their weddings, laughing, joking, drinking (on occasion a bit too much), and praying. Paul promised he would always be accessible to them and he kept his word.

When Paul rose from the kneeler the room stilled as though the Holy Spirit had entered the room.

"Like our beloved Jesus," he began, "we enter this world, we suffer its trials, and we die. But there is no reason to be afraid, because death is not an end. It's a doorway to a better life. Death marks an edge, a boundary, like," pointing to the front door, "the doorway is a boundary between the inside and outside of a house. Death is a boundary between this life and the next. It's that time in God's glorious plan when our souls are transferred from this world to the next. For some that next life is in Heaven and some need to spend time in Purgatory. But remember, Purgatory is not forever. As long as you have been a true and faithful Catholic, God, in his eternal mercy, forgives your sins and takes you up to sit at the foot of his throne. Even during your most painful trials, you can take comfort knowing that God will make all well. God will make all well."

"God will make all well," the whole group responded in unison.

I remembered Janice chastising me for not knowing that God loves us and felt a tremble. Am I a true and faithful Catholic? I wasn't sure. Would I have to go to Purgatory? Nothing in my nine years pointed to my having to be purified, to be forgiven. Besides, after what had just happened, I didn't see God making things all that well.

Where I was seated, I could see from the front room into the dining room and on into the kitchen, and as Father Paul spoke, I watched the people throughout the house. Many of the women were crying. Hadn't they heard what Father Paul had said? Ari and Chez were crying, and the tears on my mother's face glistened as the candlelight seemed to draw sparkling diamonds from them. Why were they crying? We were to take comfort. Even Uncle Julli, whom I was certain Paul was talking about, and even though Purgatory was a place of fire and purification making holy those who had not paid the price for their sins so they could grow to be worthy of sitting in the sight of God and gaze on His blessed presence, even Uncle Julli would see God. Why were they crying?

The image of the awful deathscape I saw in the bathroom the night Julli died appeared in my imagination and scared me. Could Julli be in Hell? Is that what it had meant?

I looked to his casket. He was so peaceful and undisturbed. Then he seemed to smile. The deathscape whooshed away, blown by a wind I thought I heard but didn't feel, and I saw the face of Jesus just over the top of the casket. He wasn't smiling. I checked to see if anyone else saw what I was seeing, but nothing in the room had changed. When I looked back, Jesus was gone.

"Death is not easy," Father Paul continued. "We miss the ones we love and wonder where they are. They were so much a part of our life it's like there's a hole. A very real hole. I'm sure some of you have felt it. But I want you to know the worst thing you can do. The worst thing is to try to fill it. Nothing will fill that hole except God the Father, the Son, and the Holy Ghost. You must let the Blessed Trinity fill your yearning, let the blessed Trinity take your pain, let the Blessed Trinity bring you the comfort you need to keep living in the love of Jesus.

"Remember this holy truth: the body of Julli will be resurrected. When Jesus comes again at the Last Judgment Julli's body will be joined with his soul, reunited, just like mine will, just like yours will. That's the glory of what we all have waiting for us. If we never died we would never get to that happy moment, that happy blessing, that sacred resurrection. We'd just die and our bodies would disappear in the ground. But our holy Catholic Church teaches us that our bodies will be glorified. I know this is hard to understand but believe me what I am saying is the truth from God Himself.

"When our souls rejoin our bodies on the Judgment Day they will be exalted and made majestic."

Father Paul was right, it was hard to understand. Why did we have to die to get to Heaven? If God really loves us why do we have to live this life? Why do we have to be forgiven? I looked to see what other people were doing. Many heads were bowed, others looked around. Maybe they didn't understand either.

My mother was different. She stared at Father Paul. Her face reminded me of the faces of the saints I'd seen everywhere in our church. The Brothers were not bowed, but each of them cast his gaze toward the floor.

When I turned to my father I was surprised. He had been looking at me. I felt like he wanted something from me but I didn't know what. I whispered "What?" When I did he was surprised, and with a slight jerk of his head, he turned away. Did I disappoint him again?

"At that last day," Father Paul was almost singing, "we will all see Julli again. Not in his afflictions, not his heartache, but strong and beautiful. That is a miracle. A miracle, praise God. That is the joy our Jesus has waiting for us. Eternal rest grant unto him, O Lord, and let perpetual light shine upon him. May he rest in peace."

The group responded, "May he rest in peace, Amen."

"Now it's time we turn to our great and blessed intercessor, Holy Mother Mary." Everyone knew it was now time to pray the rosary. "She enjoys the glory of Heaven but her heart aches for her children on Earth. We are her children, and like every loving mother she wants the best for us. When we pray to her she carries our words to Jesus. Jesus does not refuse His Mother Mary. He can't. So when we pray to her for Julli, Jesus himself will take your prayers right to the Father. He will take them as we pray. You must see in your hearts Jesus going right to God and asking for forgiveness for Julli. You must see that in your hearts. And when you take comfort, because you can be sure your words are reaching God's ears, reaching God's ears. So let's begin."

A stirring flowed through the house as people prepared themselves for the rosary. I never liked the rosary, fifty-three Hail Marys and six Our Fathers. That was too much. Just a few would do, I thought, if they were sincere. Was it hard for Mary to hear? If she could do what the Church said she could, why did we need to say so many?

The rosary went on for thirty minutes, and I became more and more antsy. I did everything I could to sit still, but I couldn't stop fidgeting. I saw my mother shoot her what-are-you-doing look across the room and held myself tight in place. But it wasn't long before I was squirming again. Finally the rosary ended.

"Now, let us sit in reverent silence for our dearly beloved son, our most cherished brother, and our loyal friend, God's humble servant Julli. See him sitting with God in Heaven at the foot of God's sanctified throne."

Father Paul took the empty seat next to my mother and the silence began. Several minutes into it I saw my mother take Father Paul's hand. He seemed to pull away but she held on, forcefully, hand-in-hand. They sat like that for the whole silence, my mother looking at Paul as if he were a saint.

I looked up to my father. His face was red. His eyes darted back and forth between the floor and my mother. He shifted in his seat. Just when I thought he was going to do something, Father Paul stood and announced the end of the service.

After a moment, the crowd rustled as people rose to leave. Each of them spoke to The Brothers and my mother as they left. Father Paul came to my father.

"Eddie, please take my most sincere wish for you and the pain you must feel. I know you must have cared for Julli. I will pray for him and for you."

My father nodded and Father Paul left.

I couldn't believe what I'd just heard. My father and Julli were always at each other. Except for the night when Julli died and I saw my father gently tell him to go home, they weren't friends. At least not any kind of friend I knew about. But later, as I grew older, I realized that Julli and my father were both outsiders. Julli was blood but that didn't matter. Whatever he did, it was never enough. Everyone treated him like an incompetent, so he consistently proved them right. My father wasn't blood and he could never overcome that. Julli and Eddie were actually more like brothers than The Brothers.

During the muddle of everyone's leaving, no one, not one person came to my father. I became very angry and I went to my mother and tugged at her dress.

"Look at Dad." I wanted her to see what I saw. But she wasn't available. The person she was talking with kept her attention. I tugged again but she didn't respond so I went back to my father.

I looked at Julli, laying there surrounded by flowers, candles, and the crucifix, I felt heat rise in my face. If God really does love us why did he kill his Son? Why did Jesus have to die?

My father rose and moved to the casket and, for a long time, he stared down at Julli. I saw him blink, three times, hard, and saw his lip quiver. Then he whispered, "God damn it, Julli."

I'd never heard him swear before and I was shocked.

"God damn it," he whispered again, turned and walked toward the kitchen.

I never asked him about that moment. I wanted to, but the timing never felt right. To this day I don't know what he meant.

THE END

About the Author

Jim Sniechowski was born and raised in a Catholic, working-class family in a tough Polish enclave in southwest Detroit. His grandparents arrived in Detroit from the fields and farms of Eastern Poland remaining true to a medieval sense of religiosity with its strict demand of obedience and the peasant's lifestyle they were accustomed to.

From boyhood on Jim struggled with his growing awareness of the brutality Old World Catholicism imposed on him and everyone in his community, the lower-class life they were compelled to live, including the alcohol they consumed to dull the pain they endured, and the reproach they suffered should anyone consider resisting or, even worse, leaving.

Jim, nevertheless, resisted and he was continually kept on the "to be watched" list by the nuns and priests at Our Lady Queen of Angels, his parish and elementary school. His rebellion went full force during his early teens when he joined the Royal Lancers, a local street gang.

After graduating from The University of Detroit High School, a Jesuit based college prep school, he attended the University of Detroit where he discovered the theater. After receiving rave reviews for his role as The Gentleman Caller in Tennessee Williams' *The Glass Menagerie*, once college was behind him, he was off to New York to study at The Neighborhood Playhouse in New York City and then on to a fifteen-year career as a stage actor. Jim's deep interest in character led him on to a PhD in Philosophy and Psychology and now to writing novels.

His Leaving Home Trilogy—*Worship of Hollow Gods* (first book), *An Ambition to Belong* (second book), and a forthcoming (third book) *When Angels Die*—focuses on the imprinting of early life impressions and experiences that create a mindset and lifestyle unconsciously framed and driven, gripping and animating anyone without them knowing how or why. This unconscious base produces the deepest sense of "home" and it is precisely this sense of home that must to be left behind if one is to be in possession of and live one's own life. This is the reward of a life lived with steadfast commitment and keen intention.

TO CONTACT JAMES SNIECHOWSKI

Whether for Media Interviews, Speaking Engagements, or Expert Commentary please contact James Sniechowski through:

Email: JudithandJim@judithandjim.com
Telehone: 877 810 7653

For Further information please go to:
www.JamesSniechowski.com
Website: http://www.JudithandJim.com

Acknowledgments

First and foremost, I want to acknowledge my wife Judith Sherven whose emotional presence is for me an indispensable source of strength, whose penetrating intellect keeps me alert, whose indefatigable capacity for work leaves me in awe, the depth of her love is without bottom, and also, she's just plain fun to be with. Thank You, Judith.

And of course, I must acknowledge the family into which I was born and through which I was raised. My grandparents journeyed from the ancient fields of Poland to what for them was the psychologically and spiritually wild fields of the New World—Detroit. The Old World, in which their minds and souls were immersed, was not merely confronted by the New World, of which they were naïve, it was torn apart—culturally, linguistically, religiously, practically, in all the ways they had taken for granted. Catholicism wasn't the only force insisting they have a large family. Basic survival demanded it. It was into this milieu that my uncles and aunts and my mother and father were born. The family was the core of their new life and our house was their stronghold. I salute their spirit, their blind tenacity, and what they accomplished.

I also want to thank a number of people who have participated in supporting me during the evolution of this story.

Signe Dayhoff, PhD whose incisive feedback began when she read what was then just the initial sketch and has been totally available with her writer's mind and her woman's feelings.

Kashonia Carnegie, PhD whose support has been both nurturing and directive.

Josh Domingcil who enthusiastically read an early version of the manuscript and provided many enlightening points of view, as well as answering every question I asked to help further my understanding of reader impact.

Melody Starr, our 97-year-old spiritual mother, who's been an invited member of our family for the past fifteen years and has stood by us through all of our maddening frustrations as well as celebrating with us during the many exciting delights and who never, not for one moment, ever wavered in her love and support.

Art Klein, my dear friend whose perception is unstintingly keen, whose passion is immeasurable, whose compassion is grounded in wisdom, whose eyes see from his soul, who is a mensch of the first order.

ALSO BY JAMES SNIECHOWSKI

Co-authored with Judith Sherven, PhD and
available through Amazon:
*The Heart of Marketing: Love Your Customers
and They Will Love You Back*
http://tinyurl.com/theheartofmrktg

*The New Intimacy: Discovering the Magic at the
Heart of Your Differences*
Kindle: http://tinyurl.com/k9k7f
Paperback: https://www.createspace.com/3538798

Opening to Love 365 Days a Year
http://tinyurl.com/cfbrz

Be Loved for Who You Really Are
http://tinyurl.com/dlmfc

*The Smart Couple's Guide to the Wedding of Your Dreams:
Planning Together for Less Stress and More Joy*
http://www.tinyurl.com/c8sd8

What Really Killed Whitney Houston
http://WhatReallyKilledWhitneyHouston.com

Made in the USA
San Bernardino, CA
31 March 2019